REGENTS RENAISSANCE DRAMA SERIES

General Editor: Cyrus Hoy
Advisory Editor: G. E. Bentley

THE ANTIPODES

RICHARD BROME

The Antipodes

Edited by

ANN HAAKER

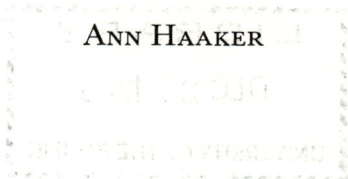

UNIVERSITY OF NEBRASKA PRESS · LINCOLN

Publishers on the Plains

UNP

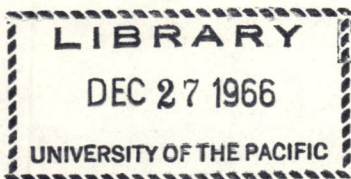

MANUFACTURED IN THE UNITED STATES OF AMERICA

Regents Renaissance Drama Series

The purpose of the Regents Renaissance Drama Series is to provide soundly edited texts, in modern spelling, of the more significant plays of the Elizabethan, Jacobean, and Caroline theater. Each text in the series is based on a fresh collation of all sixteenth- and seventeenth-century editions. The textual notes, which appear above the line at the bottom of each page, record all substantive departures from the edition used as the copy-text. Variant substantive readings among sixteenth- and seventeenth-century editions are listed there as well. In cases where two or more of the old editions present widely divergent readings, a list of substantive variants in editions through the seventeenth century is given in an appendix. Editions after 1700 are referred to in the textual notes only when an emendation originating in some one of them is received into the text. Variants of accidentals (spelling, punctuation, capitalization) are not recorded in the notes. Contracted forms of characters' names are silently expanded in speech prefixes and stage directions, and, in the case of speech prefixes, are regularized. Additions to the stage directions of the copy-text are enclosed in brackets. Stage directions such as "within" or "aside" are enclosed in parentheses when they occur in the copy-text.

Spelling has been modernized along consciously conservative lines. "Murther" has become "murder," and "burthen," "burden," but within the limits of a modernized text, and with the following exceptions, the linguistic quality of the original has been carefully preserved. The variety of contracted forms (*'em, 'am, 'm, 'um, 'hem*) used in the drama of the period for the pronoun *them* are here regularly given as *'em*, and the alternation between *a'th'* and *o'th'* (for *on* or *of the*) is regularly reproduced as *o'th'*. The copy-text distinction between preterite endings in *-d* and *-ed* is preserved except where the elision of *e* occurs in the penultimate syllable; in such cases, the final syllable is contracted. Thus, where the old editions read "threat'ned," those of the present series read "threaten'd." Where, in the old editions, a contracted preterite in *-y'd* would yield *-i'd* in modern spelling (as in "try'd," "cry'd," "deny'd"), the word is here given in its full form (e.g., "tried," "cried," "denied").

Punctuation has been brought into accord with modern practices. The effort here has been to achieve a balance between the generally light pointing of the old editions, and a system of punctuation which, without overloading the text with exclamation marks, semicolons, and dashes, will make the often loosely flowing verse (and prose) of the original syntactically intelligible to the modern reader. Dashes are regularly used only to indicate interrupted speeches, or shifts of address within a single speech.

Explanatory notes, chiefly concerned with glossing obsolete words and phrases, are printed below the textual notes at the bottom of each page. References to stage directions in the notes follow the admirable system of the Revels editions, whereby stage directions are keyed, decimally, to the line of the text before or after which they occur. Thus, a note on 0.2 has reference to the second line of the stage direction at the beginning of the scene in question. A note on 115.1 has reference to the first line of the stage direction following line 115 of the text of the relevant scene.

CYRUS HOY

University of Rochester

Contents

List of Abbreviations

Aston	Ed. Aston. *The Manners, Lawes, and Customes of all Nations*. London, 1611.
Baker	G. P. Baker, ed. *The Antipodes* in *Representative English Comedies*, Vol. III. Ed. C. M. Gayley. New York, 1914.
Bentley	Gerald Eades Bentley. *The Jacobean and Caroline Stage*. Oxford, 1941–1956.
Bullen	A. H. Bullen, ed. *The Works of Thomas Nabbes*, Vol. II. London, 1887.
Compleat	Henry Peacham. *The Compleat Gentleman*. London, 1634.
corr.	corrected
Cotgrave	R. Cotgrave. *A Dictionary of the French and English Tongues*. London, 1611.
DNB	*Dictionary of National Biography*.
Fleay	Frederick Gard Fleay. *A Biographical Chronicle of the English Drama, 1559–1642*. London, 1891.
Greg	W. W. Greg. *A Bibliography of the English Printed Drama to the Restoration*. 4 vols. Oxford, 1939–1959.
Halliwell	J. O. Halliwell. *Dictionary of Archaic and Provincial Words*. London, 1924.
Herford & Simpson	C. H. Herford and Evelyn Simpson, eds. *Ben Jonson*. Oxford, 1925–1952.
Linthicum	M. Channing Linthicum. *Costume in the Drama of Shakespeare and His Contemporaries*. Oxford, 1936.
Mandeville	*The Voyages and Travailes of Sir John Mandeville, Knight*. London, 1625.
Morgan	Appleton Morgan. *A Study in the Warwickshire Dialect*. London, 1908.
Nares	Robert Nares. *A Glossary, or Collection of Words*, ed. J. O. Halliwell and Thomas Wright. 2 vols. London, 1882.

OED	*Oxford English Dictionary.*
om.	omitted
Onions	C. T. Onions. *A Shakespeare Glossary.* Oxford, 1953.
Partridge	Eric Partridge. *Shakespeare's Bawdy.* London, 1955.
Pearson	John Pearson, ed. *Brome's Dramatic Works.* 3 vols. London, 1873.
Playford	John Playford. *The English Dancing Master.* London, 1653.
Q	Quarto of 1640
S.D.	stage direction
S.P.	speech prefix
Stow	John Stow. *The Annales of England.* London, 1631.
Strutt	Joseph Strutt. *Sports and Pastimes.* London, 1865.
Taylor	John Taylor. *All the Workes of John Taylor.* London, 1630.
Topsell	Edward Topsell. *Gesner's Historie of Foure Footed Beastes.* London, 1607.
Truth	Henry Peacham. *The Truth of Our Times.* London, 1638.
uncorr.	uncorrected
Wright	Joseph Wright. *The English Dialect Dictionary.* Oxford, 1923.

Introduction

DATE AND SOURCES

Brome contracted to compose *The Antipodes* for the Cockpit Theater in August, 1636. He wrote it during one of London's severest plagues, which began in April, 1636, and lasted until December, 1637. As a result all theaters were ordered closed from May 12, 1636, to October 2, 1637. Although Brome had signed a contract to write exclusively for the Salisbury Court Company, *The Antipodes* was intended for William Beeston, who, with his father Christopher Beeston, was starting a company of boy actors, known as Beeston's Boys, at the Cockpit Theater. In a signed note appended to the text of the 1640 quarto, Brome writes:

> *You shal find in this Booke more then was presented upon the* Stage, *and left out of the* Presentation, *for superfluous length (as some of the* Players *pretended) I thoght good al should be inserted according to the allowed* Original; *and as it was, at first, intended for the* Cock-pit Stage, *in the right of my most deserving Friend Mr.* William Beeston, *unto whom it properly appertained; and so I leave it to thy perusal, as it was generally applauded, and well acted at* Salisbury Court.

The circumstances behind this anomalous note are explained in two 1640 Requests Proceedings Documents, a complaint filed on February 12 by the Salisbury Court Company, and Richard Brome's answer of March 6 to the charges.[1] According to the documents, in April,

---

[1] I am grateful to the Huntington Library and to Professor C. W. Wallace's sister, Mrs. Victoria Berggren, for permission to use the transcriptions made on July 22, 1910, of both documents. These have been checked against a photostat of the original. The quotations are from Brome's unpublished Answer. I am particularly indebted to the late Professor Wallace and his wife as well as to the London Record Office officials not only for the exact location of the documents, but for their patient effort in making available by special treatment of the parchment those portions of Brome's answer which were badly damaged by dampness or eaten by decay. See C. W. Wallace, "Shakespere and the Blackfriars," *The Century Magazine*, LXXX (1910), 751, for the first mention of Brome's contract with Salisbury Court Theater.

1636, because of the plague in and about London, and all during the seventeen months' suspension of theatrical activity that followed, Brome was denied his usual fifteen shillings' weekly salary which had been stipulated in an earlier agreement made with the Salisbury Court Company in July, 1635. In May, 1636, the new owners of the company, according to Brome, canceled this contract, and Brome was left to shift for himself. In final desperation "in that sadd and dangerous tyme of the sicknes boeth for himself and his famyly," Brome "aboute the moneth of August then next following" solicited the aid of William Beeston, who lent him six pounds "at his need upon this defendent's Agreement to Compose and write a play for the Cockpitt Company." The Salisbury Court Company, however, reclaimed Brome's services on October 26, 1636, partially upon threats of "suites and trouble." Brome was freed from his agreement with Beeston and was promised better usage in the future. His subsequent relationship with the Salisbury Court Company remained highly unsatisfactory, throughout which time Beeston remained Brome's friend and adviser.

The Antipodes, "intended for the Cock-pit stage," is undoubtedly the play contracted for with Beeston in 1636. In Brome's summation, he reiterates: "And as to the new play which the Complainants suppose this defendent to have sould unto the said Christopher and William Beeston this defendent confesseth it to bee true that the stopage of his weekly meanes and unkind carriages aforesaid forced this defendent to contract and bargaine for the said new play with the said William Beeston but yet the said complainants and their Company had it and acted it." All this tallies with Brome's note at the end of *The Antipodes* and with the information on the title page, which states that the play was "acted in the yeare 1638 by the Queenes Majesties Servants, at Salisbury Court in Fleet-street." The limits, derived from the document, the title page, and Brome's note, date the play sometime between August, 1636, and December, 1637, when the plague had ended.

The Antipodes is a synthesis of many sources, the most important being the fantastic wonders recounted in *The Voyages and Travailes of Sir John Mandeville, Knight* (edn. 1625).[2] The dragons, monsters, varicolored animals, strange customs and manners, and all the

2 Relevant parallels from Mandeville and other current literature are recorded in the explanatory notes.

phantasmagoric lore found in Mandeville's currently popular travelogue teem in Peregrine's confused mind. A few instances of topsy-turvydom in the ordinary relations of life may have been suggested by Books Four and Five of Rabelais' *Gargantua and Pantagruel*.[3] Also evident is Brome's use of Robert Burton's *Anatomy of Melancholy*. The symptoms of melancholy afflicting the Joyless family and the cures devised for Peregrine, Joyless, and Martha can all be accounted for in Burton's widely read psychological treatise. Peregrine's illness, for example, necessitates that kind of cure classified as "artificial invention." The doctor in the play first gains Peregrine's confidence by humoring him; only then can he direct his patient's attention toward the curing "invention."[4] Burton's remedy of Martha, on the other hand, is directed toward the consummation of her marriage.[5] Her obsession for child-getting and her erotic behavior described by Joyless are similar to the symptoms of "Maids, Nunnes, and Widows Melancholy."[6]

Finally Brome borrows from numerous plays. He may still have had in mind the reversed family relations described in the first act of *The Late Lancashire Witches* (printed 1634), a play on which he collaborated with Thomas Heywood. In both *The Antipodes* and *The Late Lancashire Witches*, a son scolds a father, a waiting woman curbs a wife, a servingman counsels the master, and the maid chides a grandmother. Another play Brome certainly had in mind was *Hamlet*. There is an obvious similarity between Letoy's advice to his actors (II.ii.15–56) and Hamlet's speech to his players; both speeches are animadversions against bombastic acting and extemporaneous interpolations on the part of the actors. Clarence E. Andrews, in his *Richard Brome: A Study of His Life and Works*,[7] posits three additional

[3] E.g., catchpoles' making their livelihood by being thrashed (edn. 1694, Book IV, Ch. 12, p. 48); the Furr'd Law-Cats' presiding over the criminal courts of the Island of Condemnation where "Vice is call'd Virtue, Wickedness Piety, Treason Loyalty, Robbery Justice" (edn. 1694, Book V, Ch. 12, pp. 53–54); and finally Friar John's explaining the antipodean behavior for the Semi-quaver Friars (edn. 1694, Book V, Ch. 27, p. 134). Similar clemency is also apparent in the court scene of Thomas Randolph's *The Muses Looking Glass* (edn. 1638, IV.iii, sig. K1ᵛ) in which we have another catalogue of offenders and a Justice Milhil who for pity spares the corrupt.
[4] Robert Burton, *Anatomy of Melancholy* (edn. 1621), II.2, pp. 370–371.
[5] Burton (edn. 1638), I.3, pp. 203–204.
[6] *Ibid.*, p. 202.
[7] (New York, 1913), pp. 122–124.

plays as likely sources: (1) John Ford's *The Lover's Melancholy* (acted *c.* 1628); (2) Philip Massinger's *The Roman Actor* (acted 1626); and (3) Thomas Randolph's *The Muses Looking Glass* (acted 1630). All three employ a play within the play as a form of cure for some one of the characters, and all employ spectators who lose themselves in the action which they witness, express admiration or sympathy by verbal interpolations, and eventually merge the inner play into the main plot.

THE PLAY

Ben Jonson's young servant, Richard Brome, first attracts the notice of later generations on October 31, 1614, appropriately enough, via the words of a stage keeper. Lady Elizabeth's Men were performing Jonson's *Bartholomew Fair* at the Hope Theater. During the Induction the stage keeper suddenly interrupts his speech with: "I am looking, least the Poet [Jonson] hear me, or his man, Master Brome, behind the Arras." The allusion to the circumstances behind Brome's active participation in the theater is significant: it immediately allies Brome with Jonson and with the theater, two worthy mentors for any aspiring young playwright. Both sources of inspiration are evident in *The Antipodes*. Brome's spokesman is Letoy, lover of players and good plays, and throughout the preparation and performance of the play within a play, one can envision the young Brome watching plays take form, rehearsed, and altered to conditions; observing audience reactions at first hand; noting what constituted effective staging and effective acting. From the theater's never-ending variety, Brome could choose and assimilate. Choosing the colorful hurly-burly of London as his mecca, Anti-London, Brome in *The Antipodes* not only amasses mannerisms, prejudices, changing attitudes, and fears of London habitués, but employs all that is passing current in the theatrical chronicles of the time. Billingsgate eloquence of carmen, watermen, and sedan men vying for trade; the hypocrisy of excess Puritanism and the affectations of excess Cavalierism; the jargon of lawyers discussing lawsuits; the easy-money acquisition of projectors—the whole gamut of classes and trades is cleverly juggled in antipodal comic relief. For added variety, he combines stately processions, the noise of rabble leading a scold to the ducking pond, courtroom scenes, street scenes, and the masque.

Having served his apprenticeship under Jonson,[8] Brome was able to weave his many intrigues and assortments into a coordinated whole. From Jonson, Brome learned the technique of dramatic construction. But more important, Brome adopted Jonson's social consciousness[9] and his theory of the therapeutic value of comedy. Like Jonson, Brome delineates variations of the themes of lust and avarice as symptomatic of the illnesses of his age, which themes are basic in the play's structure. The basis of Brome's comic catharsis is explained in the Induction to Jonson's *Every Man Out of His Humor*, when Asper, Jonson's spokesman, proposes for the audience a mirror,

> As large as is the stage whereon we act,
> Where they shall see the time's deformity
> Anatomized in every nerve, and sinew
> With constant courage, and contempt of fear.

But Brome does not "scourge" his audience. He rather cajoles them, humors them, and infuses his "medicine of the mind"

> So skilfully, yet by familiar ways,
> That it begets both wonder and delight
> In his observers, while the stupid patient
> Finds health at unawares.
>
> (*The Antipodes*, I.i.25–28)

With skill and ingenuity, Brome applies Jonson's precepts to prove his own comic muse a gentle surgeon who finds the cause of the pain, heals the wound, and preserves the man.

An audience that had been restricted from all forms of diversion during twenty months of hardship and heartbreak associated with one of the nation's severest plagues needed, above all, mirth. The Joyless family, like the members of Brome's audience, have survived a plague, and in the opening scenes of the play they are welcomed into the Letoy household with promises of pleasure and entertainment

[8] Among the contemporary allusions to Brome's association with Jonson are the following: commendatory verses by C. G. in *The Antipodes* (edn. 1640), verses by John Hall and John Tatham in *The Merry Beggars* (edn. 1652), and in Ben Jonson's verses for *The Northern Lass* (edn. 1632); by Brome himself in "To my Lord of Newcastle ..." prefixed to *Covent Garden Weeded* (edn. 1659), in the Prologue to *The City Wit* (edn. 1653), and in the verses he wrote for the Beaumont and Fletcher Folio of 1647.

[9] For further study of this topic, see L. C. Knights, *Drama and Society in the Age of Jonson* (London, 1937).

to come. Determinedly gay in scene after scene of rollickingly reversed mannerisms and situations, the play parades its London stereotypes across the stage. Homespun fantasy, incorrigible slapstick, and common sense seem chaotically mixed at first until gradually reason, proper relationships, and the true comic spirit prevail. Then using one of the oldest and most conventional methods of comic resolution, the sudden discovery of hitherto unsuspected relationships of parents and children, Brome brings his play to its giddy close. Indeed, years later Samuel Pepys, detached from Brome's contemporary scene, records in his *Diary* for August 26, 1661, after seeing the play, that "there is much mirth, but no great matter else."

But mirth alone is not enough to cure the deep-seated melancholy infecting the Joyless family; it must be directed mirth. Here Brome employs his comic catharsis. To accomplish this, he introduces early in Act I the Dr. Hughball–Lord Letoy team. Conceptually, *The Antipodes* represents the successive stages of a cure effected by the combined efforts of Lord Letoy, a believer in the therapeutic value of a good play, and Dr. Hughball, a practicing psychiatrist.[10] Lawrence Babb calls *The Antipodes* little more than an attempt at a dramatization of psychiatric therapy.[11] Act I takes us through the case history, examination, diagnosis, and prescription for Peregrine's mental ailment and the concomitant ailment of his wife, and introduces us to the Dr. Hughball–Lord Letoy team. Letoy, a member of the old order of landed gentry, has somehow escaped being beggared by the times. He not only has retained his estates and household, but assumes responsibility, pays his debts, repudiates ostentation and pretension, and finds pleasure in the more wholesome diversions, whether he is in the city or country. Furthermore, he employs only home talent. His virtues, currently antipodean in themselves, are significant. As has already been noted, the Doctor's method of mind-cure for both Peregrine and his wife approximates Burton's principles for curing certain types of melancholy. Act I, then, establishes the need for both mirth and a cure. It soon becomes evident, however, that the cure is intended not only for Peregrine, a young man who has lost touch with reality, but for the entire family who act as actor-spectators

[10] R. J. Kaufmann suggests that Doctor Hughball, after Corax in Ford's *The Lover's Melancholy* (edn. 1624), is the first practicing psychiatrist to appear on the English stage (*Richard Brome, Caroline Playwright*, New York, 1961, p. 65).
[11] *Elizabethan Malady* (New York, 1951), p. 123.

in·the play, and finally for each member of the audience who in varying degrees suffers from some form of melancholy in this epidemical time.

The method, which combines "fancy" with "cure", is explained in the first scene of Act II, and is later reviewed in Act IV (scene xiii, ll. 1–21). Superficially the plan is this: Peregrine, the patient, suffers from the Mandeville hallucination and consequently lives in a world of far-fetched fantasies. The Doctor humors him, gains his confidence, and leads him to believe that he is to travel to even remoter places offering even greater mysteries than those which Mandeville visited or witnessed. The farthest place from home is Antipodes, or Anti-London. Letoy's invention makes for a spontaneous reversal of London manners, attitudes, follies, and a generous bit of nonsense which offers wonders enough for the distracted one. Furthermore, the Doctor explains that he, and later Letoy, will "interchange/ Discourse with him sometimes amidst their scenes,/ T'inform my patient" (II.i.28–30). Soon the patient finds himself engrossed in the ludicrous incongruities devised from "homebred subjects" (Prologue, l. 25), forgets Mandeville, and thereby, as explained by Letoy at the end of Act IV, is brought "As far short of a competent reason as/ He was of late beyond it" (IV.xiii.6–7). A system of comic catharsis is explained by J. L. Davis: "Comedy . . . may directly administer to human sanity generally by engrossing the mind in an elaborate scheme of incongruities and enabling it to perceive through them the omnipotence and ubiquity of imperfection."[12] As the scenes of Letoy's playlet progress, Peregrine, no longer just a spectator, begins to play an active part and soon recognizes, even in his distracted condition, a need for some kind of reform in this land of "All wit, and mirth, and good society" (I.vi.195). By Act V, Peregrine has been delivered from an existence of "Mere shadowy phantasms, or fantastic dreams" (II.iv.11) to that of a spectator, and finally to existence as an actual participant in the world about him. He is now ready for the final stage in the cure, an instructive masque "Of better settle-brain" (V.viii.47). Once his attention has been shifted from madness, or hallucination, to folly, or the foibles of society, art is ready to bring Peregrine to his proper center.

By the use of the play within the play, Brome extends his mirth-cure to members of the audience. The persistent levity and the

[12] "Richard Brome's Neglected Contribution to Comic Theory," *Studies in Philology*, XI (1943), 520 ff.

unobstrusive interplay between stereotype, fact, and imagination tend to obscure the social consciousness and the more serious implications, which, though subordinate to the intended mirth, could not but have been recognized by a contemporary audience. The cure devised for Peregrine was only an artifice. The real patients are those watching the play. From the first scene, in the catalogue of Dr. Hughball's cure, and later during the examination of the patient, and even in the antipodean scenes themselves, Brome deftly presents the many causes for the prevailing forms of melancholy—bankruptcy, corruption among "officers and men of place" (I.i.65), loveless marriages, jealousy, greed, acquisition. With an eddying thoroughness, Brome soon encompasses in scene after scene all of time's deformities stemming from lust and avarice. Beginning with family situations in Act II, he extends the situations in Acts III and IV to include individuals representative of various categories of London activities—"all/ Degrees of people, both in sex and quality" (I.vi.131–132). The play achieves *double entente*: the outer audience—the "English/ To the exterior show; but in their manners,/ Their carriage, and condition of life,/ Extremely contrary" (I.vi.110–113)—is in reality symbolically representative of the topsy-turvy conditions of the time. With tongue in cheek, Brome reminds his audience that they, like Peregrine at the beginning of the play,

> . . . count all slight that's under us, or nigh,
> And only those for worthy subjects deem,
> Fetch'd, or reach'd at (at least) from far or high,
> When low and homebred subjects have their use
> As well as those fetch'd from on high or far.
>
> (Prologue, ll. 22–26)

In the same vein he gains the audience's confidence, too, by promising a play far removed from their own play of life, so far removed "That no degree, from kaiser to the clown,/ Shall say this vice or folly was mine own" (II.v.20–21). Eventually both Peregrine and audience are dislodged from their inclination for escapism. The audience, like Peregrine, is gradually led to recognize, to be able to laugh at, and finally to criticize in true comic spirit the far-fetched spectacle of their own follies. But all is done gradually, inoffensively. Beginning with mere "frivolous nothings" (I.vi.164) like the "tittle-tattle duties" of men at home while women "Hunt, hawk, and take their pleasure" (I.vi.146–147), and cats caged from mice, ever so lightly he trips to matters of ethics and justice requiring judgment. Working from the specific to the general and from the outlandish to matters closer to home, Brome gently leads the unsuspecting guests, who, according to the plan described in Act I, will not alone be spectators "but (as we will carry it) actors/ To fill your comic scenes with double mirth" (II.i.43–44), until they eventually find "health at unawares" (I.i.28).

But life, even in Letoy's little world, is not destined to follow a set pattern. Peregrine, early in Act III, takes matters into his own hands; discord seems to prevail once again; the entertainment has to be delayed and new problems settled extempore. In the last act, however, one madness supersedes another; the illusions of Letoy's drama suddenly disappear. Peregrine leaves his world of fantasy and Martha her world of frenzy as together they partake of real life; Joyless is made to leave his imaginary world of suspicion and fears, to witness truth. In spite of Dr. Hughball's warning about presenting too many wonders at once, Letoy willingly risks delaying the cure in order that Peregrine—in fact all—may recover soundly. The play ends with two masques. An antimasque, in which Discord and her henchmen—Folly, Jealousy, Melancholy, and Madness—the breeders of common strife, take over, is followed by the main masque in which Harmony leads Mercury, Cupid, Bacchus, and Apollo—the maintainers of a commonwealth. But as in real life, and as in the plot itself, Discord, claiming a right by birth, remains defiant of the virtues. In the end, however, Harmony triumphs with "Wit against Folly, Love against Jealousy,/ Wine against Melancholy, and 'gainst Madness, Health" (V.xii.4–5).

The general concept behind the antipodean scenes is that no matter what world one seeks as an escape, the ratio between justice and injustice, folly and wisdom, good and evil, is, when realistically considered, the same. Instead of escape, Brome admonishes recognition of follies and truths in everyday life in the true comic spirit, which is to say, void of passion. Only then can wit, love, mirth, and health bring harmony and enjoyment to life. The structure of the play, moreover, becomes an integral part of its meaning. Clever manipulation of the play within the play enables Brome not only to merge two worlds of illusion into a third world of reality, but also to demonstrate concentrically the relative ratio between social consciousness and harmony: the greater the bounds of social consciousness, the greater the harmony and happiness. At the center is Letoy's

playlet for the benefit of Peregrine, the sphere of the self-centered
individual, which is set within the greater play depicting the sphere of
actor-spectators, as members of the family who must learn to cope
not only with their individual problems but with those proceeding
from the madness of others. Both worlds, finally, are set within the
still greater play, the sphere of reality, in which the audience recognizes its own part in its drama of human follies. Structurally a tour
de force, the play presents a three-level message which takes the
unsuspecting patients, the joyless ones, unawares. It is by means of
instructive entertainment, however, that each, within his own
sphere, is brought to his proper center. Thus has comedy assumed
its role as doctor of the age. This is why C. G., in his commendatory
verse, says that Jonson sojourns in Brome's *Antipodes*.

One who saw Brome's plays when first produced wrote: "In them
we see ourselves, in them we find/ Whatever time or custom taught
mankind."[13] Perhaps no other dramatist of the period gives us so
varied or so vivid a sense of the economic and moral milieu of
London, and the social consciousness of England between the
Renaissance and the Restoration.

THE TEXT

The 1640 quarto of *The Antipodes*, the only substantive edition of
the play, was printed by John Okes for Francis Constable, and was
entered in the Stationers' Register on March 19, 1640. The "allowed
original" in the appended note and the anticipatory stage directions
suggests that the copy for the quarto was almost certainly the author's
papers, or a transcript of these, which had been used as a theatrical
promptbook. The present text is based on a collation of twenty-two
of the twenty-three extant copies of Q1.[14] The press variants are
mainly concerned with changes in punctuation and a few in spelling
and spacing. In almost all cases no errors were corrected which could
not have been caught by an alert printing-house reader. Of interest is
the original proof for outer forme B (Sigs. B2^v and B4^v) of Folger
quarto, number 3, for confirmation of which I am indebted to Dr.
James G. McManaway of the Folger Shakespeare Library. The
marks represent normal printer's corrections during the printing of a

[13] T. S. in *Five New Playes* (edn. 1659), sig. A8^v.
[14] Copy No. 2 of the quarto in the Folger Shakespeare Library was in
storage, and so not available.

sheet in the Okes printing house.[15] Except for the Pearson reprint of 1873 in *The Dramatic Works of Richard Brome*, Vol. II, *The Antipodes* has been edited previously only by Professor G. P. Baker in *Representative English Comedies*, III, ed. C. M. Gayley, 1914.

ANN HAAKER

California State College at Fullerton

[15] Corrections were made in lettering and positioning of a stage direction. One mark for spacing and another, presumably for punctuation, were not corrected. For a similar proof sheet, see J. R. Brown's "A Proof-Sheet from Nicholas Okes' Printing-Shop," *Studies in Bibliography*, XI (1958), 228–321. John Okes worked in partnership with his father Nicholas Okes in 1627 and presumably took over the establishment sometime after 1638.

THE ANTIPODES

To
The Right Honorable
William, Earl Of Hertford, &c.

MY LORD:

The long experience I have had of your honor's favorable
intentions towards me hath compell'd me to this presump-
tion. But I hope your goodness will be pleased to pardon
what your benignity was the cause of, viz., the error of my
dedication. Had your candor not encourag'd me in this, I   5
had been innocent; yet, I beseech you, think not I intend it
any other than your recreation at your retirement from
your weighty employments, and to be the declaration of
your gracious encouragements towards me, and the testi-
mony of my gratitude. If the public view of the world enter-   10
tain it with no less welcome than that private one of the
stage already has given it, I shall be glad the world owes you
the thanks. If it meet with too severe construction, I hope
your protection. What hazards soever it shall justle with, my
desires are it may pleasure your lordship in the perusal,   15
which is the only ambition he is conscious of, who is,

My Lord,
Your honor's humbly devoted
RICHARD BROME

10–11. entertain it with] *Q* (*corr.*);
entertain with *Q* (*uncorr.*).

Earl of Hertford] William Seymour (1588–1660), who "loved his book
above all exercise," created Marquis of Hertford in 1640 and second Duke
of Somerset in 1660; served as governor of Prince Charles, as Privy
Councillor and later as Lord Chancellor of Oxford; dedicatee of Brome's
only extant manuscript, *The English Moore*, now at Lichfield Cathedral
Library (DNB).

5. *candor*] kindliness.

To Censuring Critics On The Approved Comedy,
The Antipodes

Jonson's alive! The world admiring stands,
And to declare his welcome there, shake hands.
Apollo's pensioners may wipe their eyes
And stifle their abortive elegies;
Taylor his goose quill may abjure again,   5
And to make paper dear, scribbling refrain;
For sure there's cause of neither. Jonson's ghost
Is not a tenant i'the Elysian coast,
But vext with too much scorn at your dispraise,
Silently stole unto a grove of bays;   10
Therefore bewail your errors, and entreat
He will return unto the former seat,
Whence he was often pleas'd to feed your ear
With the choice dainties of his theater.
But I much fear he'll not be easily won   15
To leave his bower, where grief and he alone
Do spend their time, to see how vainly we
Accept old toys for a new comedy.
Therefore repair to him, and praise each line
Of his *Volpone, Sejanus, Catiline*.   20
But stay, and let me tell you where he is:
He sojourns in his Brome's Antipodes.

C. G.

---

3. *Apollo's pensioners*] other than usual mythological significance, a possible reference to Jonson's former coterie who gathered in the "Apollo" chamber of the Old Devil Tavern.

4. *elegies*] over thirty commemorative poems by friends of Jonson, which collection was published in *Jonsonus Virbius*, ed. 1638.

5. *Taylor*] John Taylor (1580–1653), "water-poet," a Thames waterman who increased his earnings by rhyming; his publications numbered over 120.

9. *vext . . . dispraise*] The reference is to Jonson's anger expressed in his "Ode to Himselfe," appended to the 1631 octavo edition of *The New Inn*. His pique was occasioned by the failure of *The New Inn* in 1629, and later *The Magnetic Lady* in 1632 and *A Tale of a Tub* in 1633.

23. *C. G.*] Christopher Goad, member of King's Revels at Salisbury Court (Fleay, p. 169, and Baker); more likely an admirer of Ben Jonson, Charles Gerbier, author and contributor, along with Brome, to commendatory verses attached to John Tatham's *Fancies Theatre* (Bullen, p. 89). It was customary for a coterie of authors to write complimentary verses for each other.

To The Author On His Comedy,
The Antipodes

Steer'd by the hand of Fate o'er swelling seas,
Me thought I landed on th'Antipodes,
Where I was straight a stranger; for 'tis thus
Their feet do tread against the tread of us.
My scull mistook. Thy book, being in my hand,   5
Hurried my soul to th'Antipodean strand,
Where I did feast my fancy and mine eyes
With such variety of rarities,
That I perceive thy muse frequents some shade
Might be a grove for a Pierian maid.   10
Let idiots prate; it boots not what they say.
Th'Antipodes to wit and learning may
Have ample priv'lege, for among that crew
I know there's not a man can judge of you.

ROB[ERT]. CHAMBERLAIN   15

To The Author] *after Prologue in Q.*   15. ROB[ERT].   CHAMBERLAIN]   *Q*
                                                          (corr.); R.C. *Q (uncorr.).*

---

4. *Their . . . us*] "the Antipodes; the people which goe directly against us,
or with the soles of their feet against ours" (Cotgrave).

10. *Pierian maid*] a muse; Pieria in Thessaly, the reputed home of the
muses.

15. *Rob[ert] Chamberlain*] seventeenth-century writer (fl. 1640–1660)
popular among university wits when at Exeter College, Oxford, in 1637;
author of original apothegms, a comedy called *The Swaggering Damsell*
(edn. 1640), some short poems, and a collection of ancient jokes (DNB).

THE PROLOGUE

Opinion, which our author cannot court
(For the dear daintiness of it), has of late
From the old way of plays possess'd a sort
Only to run to those that carry state
In scene magnificent and language high,   5
And clothes worth all the rest, except the action.
And such are only good, those leaders cry;
And into that belief draw on a faction
That must despise all sportive, merry wit,
Because some such great play had none in it.   10

But it is known (peace to their memories)
The poets late sublimed from our age,
Who best could understand and best devise
Works that must ever live upon the stage,
Did well approve and lead this humble way,   15
Which we are bound to travail in tonight;
And though it be not trac'd so well as they
Discover'd it by true Phoebean light,
Pardon our just ambition yet that strive
To keep the weakest branch o'th' stage alive.   20

I mean the weakest in their great esteem,
That count all slight that's under us, or nigh,

---

3. *sort*] crowd.

5. *scene magnificent*] plays employing costly and elaborate masque-staging, such as William Strode's *The Floating Island* (edn. 1636), William Cartwright's *The Royal Slave* (edn. 1636) and *The Lady Errant* (edn. 1637), and Sir John Suckling's *Aglaura* (edn. 1637).

6. *clothes ... rest*] Concerning *Aglaura*, George Gerrard wrote to the Earl of Strafford, February 7, 1637/8: "Sutlin's Play cost three or four hundred Pounds setting out, eight or ten Suits of new Cloaths he gave the Players; an unheard of Prodigality" (*Strattforde's Letters*, II, 150; in Bentley, V, 1202).

12. *poets late sublimed*] certainly Jonson, who died in 1637; possibly Dekker, who died in 1632, and Chapman, who died in 1634.

20. *weakest branch*] plays modeled after those of Jonson and the older poets, the popularity of which was superseded by the current fad for spectacle, love-and-honor plays, and romantic tragicomedies.

And only those for worthy subjects deem,
Fetch'd, or reach'd at (at least) from far or high,
When low and homebred subjects have their use   25
As well as those fetch'd from on high or far;
And 'tis as hard a labor for the muse
To move the earth as to dislodge a star.
See yet those glorious plays, and let their sight
Your admiration move; these, your delight.   30

---

30. *admiration*] wonder.

THE PERSONS IN THE PLAY

BLAZE, *an herald painter*
JOYLESS, *an old country gentleman*
HUGHBALL, *a Doctor of Physic*
BARBARA, *wife to Blaze*
MARTHA, *wife to Peregrine*   5
LETOY, *a fantastic lord*
QUAILPIPE, *his curate*
PEREGRINE, *son to Joyless*
DIANA, *wife to Joyless*
BYPLAY, *a conceited servant to Letoy*   10
TRUELOCK, *a close friend to Letoy*
FOLLOWERS OF THE LORD LETOY'S, *who are actors in the byplay*

---

1. *herald painter*] "A Herald Painter is such as Paints Coats of Arms on
Escochions, Shields, Tables, Penons; Standarts, and such like" (*OED*,
quoting R. Holme).

6. *fantastic*] highly imaginative as well as eccentric.

7. *Quailpipe*] a small whistle used by fowlers to allure quails.

10. *conceited*] clever, amusing, and fastidious.

The Antipodes

[Enter] Blaze *[and]* Joyless.

BLAZE.

    To me, and to the city, sir, you are welcome,
    And so are all about you: we have long
    Suffer'd in want of such fair company.
    But now that time's calamity has given way
    (Thanks to high Providence) to your kinder visits,   5
    We are (like half pin'd wretches that have lain
    Long on the planks of sorrow, strictly tied
    To a forc'd abstinence from the sight of friends)
    The sweetlier fill'd with joy.
JOYLESS.   Alas, I bring
    Sorrow too much with me to fill one house   10
    In the sad number of my family.
BLAZE.

    Be comforted, good sir; my house, which now
    You may be pleas'd to call your own, is large
    Enough to hold you all; and for your sorrows,
    You came to lose 'em; and I hope the means   15
    Is readily at hand. The doctor's coming,
    Who, as by letters I advertis'd you,
    Is the most promising man to cure your son
    The kingdom yields. It will astonish you
    To hear the marvels he hath done in cures   20
    Of such distracted ones as is your son,
    And not so much by bodily physic (no,
    He sends few recipes to th'apothecaries)

---

   3. *Suffer'd in want*] endured the absence.
   4. *time's calamity*] refers to the plague and the closing of the theaters from May 12, 1636, to October 2, 1637, except for the week of February 24 to March 1.
   6. *pin'd*] wasted away as with hunger.

As medicine of the mind, which he infuses
So skilfully, yet by familiar ways,   25
That it begets both wonder and delight
In his observers, while the stupid patient
Finds health at unawares.

JOYLESS.   You speak well of him;
Yet I may fear my son's long-grown disease
Is such he hath not met with.

BLAZE.   Then I'll tell you, sir,   30
He cur'd a country gentleman that fell mad
For spending of his land before he sold it:
That is, 'twas sold to pay his debts. All went
That way for a dead horse, as one would say:
He had not money left to buy his dinner   35
Upon that wholesale day. This was a cause
Might make a gentleman mad, you'll say; and him
It did, as mad as landless squire could be.
This doctor by his art remov'd his madness
And mingled so much wit among his brains   40
That, by the overflowing of it merely,
He gets and spends five hundred pound a year now
As merrily as any gentleman
In Derbyshire. I name no man; but this
Was pretty well, you'll say.

JOYLESS.   My son's disease   45
Grows not that way.

BLAZE.   There was a lady mad,
I name no lady: but stark mad she was
As any in the country, city, or almost
In court could be.

JOYLESS.   How fell she mad?

BLAZE.   With study,
Tedious and painful study. And for what   50
Now, can you think?

JOYLESS.   For painting, or new fashions?

---

27. *stupid*] stunned.

34. *for . . . horse*] with no hope of receiving further profit (*OED*).

51. *painting*] art of applying make-up, common practice among women
in the seventeenth century which sometimes in using "many a secret thing"
required "fourteene hours" (*Choice, Chance, and Change*, edn. 1606, sig. K2).

I cannot think for the philosopher's stone.

BLAZE.

    No, 'twas to find a way to love her husband,
    Because she did not, and her friends rebuk'd her.

JOYLESS.

    Was that so hard to find, if she desir'd it?   55

BLAZE.

    She was seven years in search of it, and could not,
    Though she consum'd his whole estate by it.

JOYLESS.

    'Twas he was mad then.

BLAZE.   No, he was not born
    With wit enough to lose; but mad was she
    Until this doctor took her into cure;   60
    And now she lies as lovingly on a flockbed
    With her own knight as she had done on down
    With many others, but I name no parties.
    Yet this was well, you'll say.

JOYLESS.   Would all were well!

BLAZE.

    Then, sir, of officers and men of place,   65
    Whose senses were so numb'd they understood not
    Bribes from due fees, and fell on praemunires,
    He has cur'd divers, that can now distinguish
    And know both when and how to take of both,
    And grow most safely rich by't. T'other day   70
    He set the brains of an attorney right,
    That were quite topsy-turvy overturn'd
    In a pitch o'er the bar, so that (poor man)
    For many moons he knew not whether he
    Went on his heels or's head, till he was brought   75

---

52. *philosopher's stone*] preparation supposed by alchemists to possess the property of changing other metals to gold or silver, to prolong life indefinitely, and to cure all wounds and diseases (*OED*).

61. *flockbed*] bed stuffed with tufts or particles of wool and cotton.

67. *praemunires*] "a writ by which the sheriff is charged to summon a person accused, originally, of prosecuting in a foreign court a suit cognizable by the law of England, and later, of asserting or maintaining papal jurisdiction in England, thus denying the ecclesiastical supremacy of the sovereign" (*OED*).

68. *divers*] several.

To this rare doctor; now he walketh again
As upright in his calling as the boldest
Amongst 'em. This was well, you'll say.

JOYLESS.   'Tis much.

BLAZE.

And then for horn-mad citizens, my neighbours,
He cures them by the dozens, and we live   80
As gently with our wives as rams with ewes.

JOYLESS.

We do, you say. Were you one of his patients?

BLAZE [aside].

'Slid, he has almost catch'd me.—No, sir, no;
I name no parties, I, but wish you merry.
I strain to make you so, and could tell forty   85
Notable cures of his to pass the time
Until he comes.

JOYLESS.   But, pray, has he the art
To cure a husband's jealousy?

BLAZE.

Mine, sir, he did— [Aside.] 'Sfoot, I am catch'd again.

JOYLESS.

But still you name no party. Pray, how long,   90
Good Master Blaze, has this so famous doctor,
Whom you so well set out, been a professor?

BLAZE.

Never in public; nor endures the name
Of doctor, though I call him so, but lives
With an odd lord in town, that looks like no lord.   95
My doctor goes more like a lord than he.

Enter Doctor.

Oh, welcome, sir. I sent mine own wife for you.
Ha' you brought her home again?

96.1. *Enter*] *Baker; Ex. Q.*

---

79. *horn-mad*] madness caused by fear of being cuckolded.
83. *'Slid*] common seventeenth-century oath, "God's lid" (eyelid).
89. *'Sfoot*] oath, "Christ's foot."
92. *professor*] i.e., in the profession.

[I.ii]   Blaze, Doctor, Joyless.

DOCTOR.

She's in your house
With gentlewomen who seem to lodge here.

BLAZE.

Yes, sir, this gentleman's wife and his son's wife.
[*Aside to* Doctor.]   They all ail something, but his son, 'tis
    thought,
Is falling into madness, and is brought   5
Up by his careful father to the town here
To be your patient. Speak with him about it.

DOCTOR [*to* Joyless].

How do you find him, sir? Does his disease
Take him by fits, or is it constantly
And at all times the same?

JOYLESS.   For the most part   10
It is only inclining still to worse
As he grows more in days; by all the best
Conjectures we have met with in the country,
'Tis found a most deep melancholy.

DOCTOR.

Of what years is he?

JOYLESS.   Of five and twenty, sir.   15

DOCTOR.

Was it born with him? Is it natural
Or accidental? Have you or his mother
Been so at any time affected?

JOYLESS.   Never.
Not she unto her grave, nor I till then,
Knew what a sadness meant; though since, I have   20
In my son's sad condition, and some crosses
In my late marriage, which at further time
I may acquaint you with.

BLAZE [*aside*].   The old man's jealous

---

6. *careful*] sorrowful.
16. *natural*] inherited.
17. *accidental*] by chance circumstance, environmental.

Of his young wife! I find him by the question
He put me to ere while.
DOCTOR.   Is your son married?   25
JOYLESS.
Divers years since; for we had hope a wife
Might have restrain'd his traveling thoughts, and so
Have been a means to cure him, but it fail'd us.
DOCTOR.
What has he in his younger years been most
Addicted to? What study, or what practice?   30
JOYLESS.
You have now, sir, found the question which, I think,
Will lead you to the ground of his distemper.
DOCTOR.
That's the next way to the cure. Come quickly, quickly.
JOYLESS.
In tender years he always lov'd to read
Reports of travels and of voyages;   35
And when young boys like him would tire themselves
With sports and pastimes, and restore their spirits
Again by meat and sleep, he would whole days
And nights (sometimes by stealth) be on such books
As might convey his fancy round the world.   40
DOCTOR.
Very good; on.
JOYLESS.   When he grew up towards twenty,
His mind was all on fire to be abroad;
Nothing but travel still was all his aim;
There was no voyage or foreign expedition
Be said to be in hand, but he made suit   45
To be made one in it. His mother and
Myself oppos'd him still in all and, strongly
Against his will, still held him in and won
Him into marriage, hoping that would call
In his extravagant thoughts; but all prevail'd not,   50

---

30. *study*] employment.
33. *next way*] shortest, most direct way.
42. *mind . . . fire*] a brain fever, monomania for travel.
50. *extravagant*] wandering.

Nor stay'd him, though at home, from traveling
So far beyond himself that now, too late,
I wish he had gone abroad to meet his fate.
DOCTOR.
Well, sir, upon good terms I'll undertake
Your son. Let's see him.
JOYLESS.   Yet there's more: his wife, sir.   55
DOCTOR.
I'll undertake her, too. Is she mad, too?
BLAZE.
They'll ha' mad children then.
DOCTOR.   Hold you your peace.
JOYLESS.
Alas, the danger is they will have none.
He takes no joy in her, and she no comfort
In him; for though they have been three years wed,   60
They are yet ignorant of the marriage bed.
DOCTOR.
I shall find her the madder of the two, then.
JOYLESS.
Indeed, she's full of passion, which she utters
By the effects, as diversely as several
Objects reflect upon her wand'ring fancy,   65
Sometimes in extreme weepings, and anon
In vehement laughter; now in sullen silence,
And presently in loudest exclamations.
DOCTOR.
Come, let me see 'em, sir; I'll undertake
Her, too. Ha' you any more? How does your wife?   70
JOYLESS.
Some other time for her.
DOCTOR.   I'll undertake
Her, too. And you yourself, sir (by your favor,
And some few yellow spots which I perceive
About your temples), may require some counsel.

---

54. *undertake*] guarantee to cure (*OED*).
58. *danger*] difficulty.
64. *several*] different.
73. *yellow spots*] signs of jealousy.

[I.iii]   *Enter* Barbara.

BLAZE [*aside*].

    So, he has found him.
JOYLESS.   But my son, my son, sir!
BLAZE.

    Now, Bab, what news?
BARBARA.   There's news too much within
    For any homebred, Christian understanding.
JOYLESS.

    How does my son?
BARBARA.   He is in travail, sir.
JOYLESS.

    His fit's upon him?
BARBARA.   Yes. Pray, Doctor Hughball,   5
    Play the man-midwife and deliver him
    Of his huge timpany of news—of monsters,
    Pigmies, and giants, apes, and elephants,
    Griffins, and crocodiles, men upon women,
    And women upon men, the strangest doings—   10
    As far beyond all Christendom as 'tis to't.
DOCTOR.

    How, how?
BARBARA.   Beyond the moon and stars, I think,
    Or Mount in Cornwall either.
BLAZE.

    How prettily like a fool she talks!

---

2. *news*] (1) tidings; (2) novelties.
4. *travail*] (1) travel; (2) labor in childbirth.
7. *timpany*] morbid swelling; here used figuratively in reference to pregnancy.
7–10. *monsters . . . men*] as described in Mandeville, I.vi.26, *n.*
8. *Pigmies*] Mandeville, Chap. LXIV, sig. O4ᵛ.
8. *giants*] Mandeville, Chap. XCII, sig. S2ᵛ.
8. *apes*] Mandeville, Chap. LXIII, sig. O4ᵛ.
8. *elephants*] Mandeville, Chap. XCIX, sig. T2.
9. *Griffins*] Mandeville, Chap. LXXXV, sigs. R2ᵛ–R3.
9. *crocodiles*] Mandeville, Chap. XCIV, sig. S3ᵛ.
9. *men upon women*] Mandeville, Chap. LXII, sig. O3ᵛ.
13. *Mount in Cornwall*] St. Michael's Mount.
14. *prettily*] cleverly.

And she were not mine own wife, I could be   15
So taken with her.
DOCTOR.   'Tis most wondrous strange.
BARBARA.

He talks much of the kingdom of Cathaya,
Of one great Khan and Goodman Prester John
(Whate'er they be), and says that Khan's a clown
Unto the John he speaks of; and that John   20
Dwells up almost at Paradise. But sure his mind
Is in a wilderness, for there he says
Are geese that have two heads apiece, and hens
That bear more wool upon their backs than sheep—
DOCTOR.
Oh, Mandeville. Let's to him. Lead the way, sir.   25
BARBARA.
And men with heads like hounds!
DOCTOR.   Enough, enough.

---

18. *Khan*] emperor of Cathay (Mandeville, Chap. LXVII–LXXV, sigs. P2ᵛ–Q2).
18. *Prester John*] mentioned in Mandeville (Chap. XCIX, sig. T2); also in Aston (sigs. C3ᵛ–C4): "that the King of Aethiopia (whome wee call Pretoian or Presbiter Joan . . .) is so potent a Prince, that hee is sayd to have under him as his vassalls three-score and two Kings. And that all their great Bishops and states of all those kingdomes, are wholy guided by him, at whose hands the order of Priesthood is obtained, which authority was by the Pope of Rome given and annexed to the Majesty of their Kings, and yet Hee himselfe is no Priest, nor never entred into any holy orders."
19. *Khan's a clown*] Here Brome departs from the Mandeville version: "This great Canne is the mightiest Lord of the world, for Prester John is not so great a Lord as he . . ." (Chap. LXXV, sig. Q2).
21. *Paradise*] "Men say that Paradise terrestre is the highest land of all the world . . ." (Mandeville, Chap. CII, sig. T3).
23. *geese*] Mandeville, Chap. LXI, sig. O1.
23. *hens*] Mandeville, Chap. LXIII, sig. O4.
25. *Mandeville*] John Mandeville (1300–1372) left England in 1327 and after thirty-three years of remarkable adventures fighting infidels, serving the Sultan of Egypt, living three years in Peking, the residence of the Great Khan, returned to his country and wrote an account of his travels in "the yeere of our Lord 1364 . . . for the pleasure of all such as delight to reade the strange and wonderfull mervailes of other forraine Countries, as also for a direction to all such as shall desire to see either all, or some of these Countries heretofore specified" (Sig. U2).
26. *heads . . . hounds*] Mandeville, Chap. LXI, sig. N4ᵛ.

BARBARA.

    You'll find enough within, I warrant ye.

                    Exeunt [Doctor, Blaze, *and* Joyless].

[I.iv]   *Enter* Martha.

BARBARA.

    And here comes the poor, mad gentleman's wife,
    Almost as mad as he. She haunts me all
    About the house to impart something to me.
    Poor heart, I guess her grief, and pity her.
    To keep a maidenhead three years after marriage   5
    Under wedlock and key! Insufferable, monstrous!
    It turns into a wolf within the flesh,
    Not to be fed with chickens and tame pigeons.
    I could wish maids be warn'd by't not to marry
    Before they have wit to lose their maidenheads   10
    For fear they match with men whose wits are past it.
    What a sad look! And what a sigh was there!—
    Sweet Mistress Joyless, how is't with you now?

MARTHA.

    When I shall know, I'll tell. Pray tell me first,
    How long have you been married?

BARBARA [*aside*].   Now she is on it.—   15

    Three years, forsooth.

MARTHA.   And, truly, so have I;

    We shall agree, I see.

BARBARA.   If you'll be merry.

MARTHA.

    No woman merrier, now I have met with one
    Of my condition. Three years married, say you? Ha, ha, ha!

BARBARA.

    What ails she, trow?

27.1.] *Ex. 3. Q.*   [I.iv] *Scene division om. Q.*

---

   7. *wolf . . . flesh*] a cancerous sore. "There is a disease called a wolfe, because it consumeth and eateth up the flesh in the bodie next the sore, and must every day be fed with fresh meat, as Lambes, Pigeons, and such other things wherein is bloode, or else it consumeth al the flesh of the body, leaving not so much as the skin to cover the bones" (Topsell, sig. Xxxi^v, quoted in John Webster, *The White Devil*, ed. J. R. Brown [Cambridge, Mass., 1960], p. 145).
   20. *trow*] do you suppose.

MARTHA.   Three years married! Ha, ha, ha!   20
BARBARA.
    Is that a laughing matter?
MARTHA.   'Tis just my story,
    And you have had no child. That's still my story. Ha, ha, ha!
BARBARA.
    Nay, I have had two children.
MARTHA.   Are you sure on't,
    Or does your husband only tell you so?
    Take heed o' that, for husbands are deceitful.   25
BARBARA.
    But I am o'the surer side. I am sure
    I groan'd for mine and bore 'em, when at best
    He but believes he got 'em.
MARTHA.   Yet both he
    And you may be deceiv'd, for now I'll tell you,
    My husband told me, fac'd me down and stood on't,   30
    We had three sons, and all great travelers—
    That one had shook the great Turk by the beard.
    I never saw 'em, nor am I such a fool
    To think that children can be got and born,
    Train'd up to men, and then sent out to travel,   35
    And the poor mother never know nor feel
    Any such matter. There's a dream indeed!
BARBARA.
    Now you speak reason, and 'tis nothing but
    Your husband's madness that would put that dream
    Into you.
MARTHA.   He may put dreams into me, but   40
    He ne'er put child, nor anything towards it yet,
    To me to making. Something, sure, belongs   *Weep.*
    To such a work; for I am past a child,
    Myself, to think they are found in parsley beds,
    Strawberry banks, or rosemary bushes, though   45

---

32. *great Turk*] Murad IV (1623–1640), sultan of Turkey, notorious for one of the bloodiest of reigns.

44. *parsley beds*] "The child, when new-born, comes out of the parsley bed, they will say in the North" (quoted in *OED*).

45. *rosemary*] emblem of remembrance, used at both funerals and weddings.

I must confess I have sought and search'd such places,
Because I would fain have had one.

BARBARA [*aside*].   'Las, poor fool!

MARTHA.

Pray tell me, for I think nobody hears us,
How came you by your babes? I cannot think
Your husband got them you.

BARBARA [*aside*].   Fool, did I say?   50
She is a witch, I think.—Why not my husband?
Pray, can you charge me with another man?

MARTHA.

Nor with him neither. Be not angry, pray now;
For were I now to die, I cannot guess
What a man does in child-getting. I remember   55
A wanton maid once lay with me, and kiss'd
And clipp'd and clapp'd me strangely, and then wish'd
That I had been a man to have got her with child.
What must I then ha' done, or (good now, tell me)
What has your husband done to you?

BARBARA [*aside*].   Was ever   60
Such a poor piece of innocence three years married!—
Does not your husband use to lie with you?

MARTHA.

Yes, he does use to lie with me, but he does not
Lie with me to use me as he should, I fear;
Nor do I know to teach him. Will you tell me?   65
I'll lie with you and practice, if you please.
Pray take me for a night or two, or take
My husband and instruct him but one night.
Our country folks will say you London wives
Do not lie every night with your own husbands.   70

BARBARA.

Your country folks should have done well to ha' sent
Some news by you! But I trust none told you there,
We use to leave our fools to lie with madmen.

64. he] *Baker;* she *Q.*

---

47. *fain*] willingly.
57. *clipp'd and clapp'd*] embraced and fondled passionately.

MARTHA.

Nay, now again y'are angry.

BARBARA.   No, not I,

But rather pity your simplicity.   75

Come, I'll take charge and care of you—

MARTHA.   I thank you.

BARBARA.

—And wage my skill against my doctor's art

Sooner to ease you of these dangerous fits

Than he shall rectify your husband's wits.

MARTHA.

Indeed, indeed, I thank you.   *Exeunt.*   80

[I.v]   [*Enter*] Letoy [*and*] Blaze.

LETOY.

Why, broughtst thou not mine arms and pedigree

Home with thee, Blaze, mine honest herald's painter?

BLAZE.

I have not yet, my lord, but all's in readiness

According to the herald's full directions.

LETOY.

But has he gone to the root; has he deriv'd me   5

Ex origine, ab antiquo? Has he fetch'd me

Far enough, Blaze?

BLAZE.   Full four descents beyond

The conquest, my good lord, and finds that one

Of your French ancestry came in with the Conqueror.

LETOY.

Jeffrey Letoy; 'twas he from whom the English   10

Letoys have our descent, and here have took

Such footing that we'll never out while France

---

80. S.D.] *Q prints in margin beside
l. 79.*

---

77. *art*] professional skill.
[I.v]
4. *herald's*] "The Herald's College, instituted in the fifteenth century, consisted of the earl marshal, three kings-at-arms, six heralds, and three pursuivants. Its chief business is granting armorial bearings or coats of arms, and tracing and preserving genealogies" (Baker).

Is France, and England England,
And the sea passable to transport a fashion:
My ancestors and I have been beginners   15
Of all new fashions in the court of England
From before *Primo Ricardi Secundi*
Until this day.

BLAZE.   I cannot think, my lord,
They'll follow you in this though.

LETOY.   Mark the end.
I am without a precedent for my humor.   20
But is it spread, and talk'd of in the town?

BLAZE.
It is, my lord, and laugh'd at by a many.

LETOY.
I am more beholding to them than all the rest;
Their laughter makes me merry; others' mirth,
And not mine own it is, that feeds me, that   25
Battens me as poor men's cost does usurers.
But tell me, Blaze, what say they of me, ha?

BLAZE.
They say, my lord, you look more like a pedlar
Than like a lord, and live more like an emperor.

LETOY.
Why, there they ha' me right: let others shine   30
Abroad in cloth o' bodkin; my broadcloth
Pleases mine eye as well, my body better.
Besides, I'm sure 'tis paid for (to their envy).
I buy with ready money; and at home here

23. S.P.] *Baker; om. in Q, where   Blaze's preceding speech.*
ll. 23–27 are printed as part of

---

14. *transport a fashion*] cf. Peacham's allusion to the fashion-minded
English who above nations "doat upon new fasions" and "when one is
growne stale runne presently over into *France*, to seeke a new, making that
noble and flourishing kingdome the magazin of our fooleries" (*Truth*,
pp. 73–74).
17. *Primo Ricardi Secundi*] i.e., 1377.
19. *this*] this fashion or conceit.
20. *humor*] in the Jonsonian sense.   26. *Battens*] fattens.
31. *bodkin*] baudekin, a richly embroidered cloth originally made with
warp of gold thread and woof of silk.

With as good meat, as much magnificence,   35
As costly pleasures, and as rare delights,
Can satisfy my appetite and senses
As they with all their public shows and braveries.
They run at ring and tilt 'gainst one another;
I and my men can play a match at football,   40
Wrestle a handsome fall, and pitch the bar,
And crack the cudgels, and a pate sometimes,
'Twould do you good to see't.

BLAZE.   More than to feel't.

LETOY.

They hunt the deer, the hare, the fox, the otter,
Polecats, or harlots, what they please, whilst I   45
And my mad grigs, my men, can run at base,
And breathe ourselves at barley-break and dancing.

BLAZE.

Yes, my lord, i'th' country, when you are there.

LETOY.

And now I am here i'th' city, sir, I hope
I please myself with more choice home delights,   50
Than most men of my rank.

BLAZE.   I know, my lord,
Your house in substance is an amphitheater
Of exercise and pleasure.

LETOY.   Sir, I have
For exercises, fencing, dancing, vaulting,
And for delight, music of all best kinds;   55
Stageplays and masques are nightly my pastimes,

---

41. *pitch the bar*] a favorite sport among the nobility until the seventeenth century, when it became a diversion mainly for soldiers and common people.

46. *mad grigs*] "an extravagantly lively person, one who is full of frolic and jest" (*OED*).

46. *run at base*] prisoner's base, a common country recreation.

47. *barley-break*] "An old country game varying in different parts, but somewhat resembling *Prisoner's Bars*, originally played by six persons (three of each sex) in couples; one couple, being left in the middle den termed 'hell,' had to catch the others, who were allowed to separate or 'break when hard pressed, and thus to change partners, but had when caught to take their turn as catchers'" (*OED*).

And all within myself: my own men are
My music and my actors. I keep not
A man or boy but is of quality:
The worst can sing or play his part o'th' viols   60
And act his part, too, in a comedy,
For which I lay my bravery on their backs;
And where another lord undoes his followers,
I maintain mine like lords. And there's my bravery.

Hoboys. A service as for dinner, pass over the stage, borne by many servitors
richly apparel'd, doing honor to Letoy as they pass.   *Exeunt.*

Now tell me, Blaze, look these like pedlars' men?   65
BLAZE.
Rather an emperor's, my lord.
LETOY.   I tell thee,
These lads can act the emperors' lives all over,
And Shakespeare's chronicled histories, to boot;
And were that Caesar or that English Earl
That lov'd a play and player so well now living,   70
I would not be outvied in my delights.
BLAZE.   My lord, 'tis well.
LETOY.
I love the quality of playing: ay, I love a play with all
My heart, a good one; and a player that is
A good one, too, with all my heart. As for the poets,
No men love them, I think, and therefore   75
I write all my plays myself, and make no doubt
Some of the court will follow
Me in that, too. Let my fine lords
Talk o' their horse tricks, and their jockies that
Can outtalk them. Let the gallants boast   80

72. ay, I] *this edn.;* I, J Q.

___

64.1. *Hoboys*] hautboys, instruments akin to the modern oboe.
69. *Caesar*] Nero, in reference to his patronage of theatrical spectacles.
69. *English Earl*] presumably the Earl of Leicester, under whose patronage
the actors first gained in 1576 a permanent home in London at The Theatre.
72. *quality*] actor's profession.
78. *that, too*] an allusion to the courtier dramatists. In the epilogue to
Brome's *Court Beggar* (edn. 1653), Brome accused them of buying their plays
from University scholars.

Their May-games, play-games, and their mistresses;
I love a play in my plain clothes, ay,
And laugh upon the actors in their brave ones.

Enter Quailpipe.

QUAILPIPE.

My lord, your dinner stays prepar'd.

LETOY.   Well, well,
Be you as ready with your grace as I   85
Am for my meat, and all is well. Blaze, we have rambled
                                        Exit Quailpipe.
From the main point this while: it seems by his letter,
My doctor's busy at thy house. I know who's there,
Beside. Give him this ring. Tell him it wants
A finger. Farewell, good Blaze.   [*Exit* Letoy.]   90

BLAZE.

Tell him it wants a finger? My small wit
Already finds what finger it must fit.   [*Exit* Blaze.]

[I.vi]   *Enter* Doctor, Peregrine, *a book in his hand*, Joyless, Diana.

DOCTOR.

Sir, I applaud your noble disposition,
And even adore the spirit of travel in you,
And purpose to wait on it through the world,
In which I shall but tread again the steps
I heretofore have gone.   5

PEREGRINE.

All the world o'er ha' you been already?

DOCTOR.

Over and under, too.

PEREGRINE.   In the Antipodes?

DOCTOR.

Yes, through, and through;
No isle nor angle in that nether world
But I have made discovery of. Pray, sir, sit.   10
[*To* Joyless.]   And, sir, be you attentive; I will warrant

84. S.P. QUAILPIPE.] *Baker;* Re. (*i.e.,*   86.1.] *Q prints in margin at right of*
Retainer) *Q.*   *l. 85.*

---

83. *brave*] splendid, showy.

His speedy cure without the help of Galen,
Hippocrates, Avicen, or Dioscorides.

DIANA.

A rare man! Husband, truly I like his person
As well as his rare skill.

JOYLESS.   Into your chamber!   15
I do not like your liking of men's persons.

DOCTOR.

Nay, lady, you may stay. Hear and admire,
If you so please, but make no interruptions.

JOYLESS [*aside to* Diana].

And let no looser words, or wand'ring look,
Bewray an intimation of the slight   20
Regard you bear your husband, lest I send you
Upon a further pilgrimage than he
Feigns to convey my son.

DIANA.   Oh jealousy!

DOCTOR.

Do you think, sir, to th' Antipodes such a journey?

PEREGRINE.

I think there's none beyond it; and that Mandeville,   25
Whose excellent work this is, was th'only man
That e'er came near it.

DOCTOR.   Mandeville went far.

PEREGRINE.

Beyond all English legs that I can read of.

DOCTOR.

What think you, sir, of Drake, our famous countryman?

PEREGRINE.

Drake was a didapper to Mandeville.   30

---

12. *Galen*] Greek physician and philosophical writer (*c.* 130–200 A.D.).

13. *Hippocrates*] the founder of Greek medical science (*c.* 460–*c.* 377 B.C.).

13. *Avicen*] correctly, Ibn-Sina (980–1037 A.D.), the greatest of early Muslim philosophers and the most celebrated Arabian physician.

13. *Dioscorides*] first-century Greek physician. (Fl. *c.* 50 A.D.).

26. *work*] *The Voyages and Travailes of Sir John Mandeville Knight, Wherein is set downe the Way to the Holy Land, and to Hierusalem: As also to the Lands of the great Canne, and of Praester John, Inde, and divers other Countries: together with the many and strange Mervailes therein* (edn. 1625).

30. *didapper*] dabchick, word play on "drake"; hence in comparison, "unimportant."

Candish, and Hawkyns, Furbisher, all our voyagers
Went short of Mandeville. But had he reach'd

[*Turns pages in book.*]

To this place here—yes, here—this wilderness,
And seen the trees of the sun and moon, that speak
And told King Alexander of his death, he then   35
Had left a passage ope for travelers
That now is kept and guarded by wild beasts—
Dragons, and serpents, elephants white and blue,
Unicorns, and lions of many colors,
And monsters more, as numberless as nameless.   40

DOCTOR.
    Stay there—
PEREGRINE.   Read here else. Can you read?
    Is it not true?
DOCTOR.   No truer than I ha' seen't.
DIANA.
    Ha' you been there, sir? Ha' you seen those trees?
DOCTOR.
    And talk'd with 'em, and tasted of their fruit.
PEREGRINE.
    Read here again then: it is written here   45

---

31. *Candish ... Furbisher*] "Peregrine selects the first and the second
Englishman to circumnavigate the globe, Drake and Cavendish; a third,
Richard Hawkyns, who started to go round the world, but died off Porto
Rico; and the first English Arctic explorer, Martin Frobisher" (Baker).

33. *wilderness*] the wilderness surrounding the Paradise Terrestre
described in Mandeville (Chap. CIII, sig. T3ᵛ).

34-46. *trees ... year*] cf. Mandeville (Chap. XCIX, sig. T2): "In this
wildernesse ... are the trees of the Sunne, and of the Moone, that speke to
King Alexander, and told him of his death, and men say, that those that
keepe those trees and eat of the fruits of them, live foure or five hundred
yeere through vertue of the fruit, and wee would gladly have gone thither,
but I thinke that an hundred thousand men of armes could not passe that
wildernesse for the plentie of wilde beasts, as Dragons, and Serpents, that
slay men when they passe that way. In this land are many Elephants, both
white and blue, without number, & Unicornes, and Lyons of many colours."

34. *speak*] Professor Baker emends this to "spoke" according to the passage
from Chap. XCIX of the 1887 edition of Mandeville (ed. John Ashton):
"spoke to Kyng Alexander." The 1625 edition of Mandeville, however,
reads: "that speke to King Alexander."

41. *else*] if you do not believe (*OED*).

That you may live four or five hundred year.
DIANA.

Brought you none of that fruit home with you, sir?
JOYLESS.

You would have some of't, would you, to have hope
T'outlive your husband by't?
DIANA.   I'd ha't for you,
In hope you might outlive your jealousy.   50
DOCTOR.

Your patience both, I pray; I know the grief
You both do labor with, and how to cure it.
JOYLESS.

Would I had given you half my land, 'twere done.
DIANA.

Would I had given him half my love, to settle
The t'other half free from incumbrances   55
Upon my husband.
DOCTOR.   Do not think it strange, sir:
I'll make your eyes witnesses of more
Than I relate, if you'll but travel with me.
You hear me not deny that all is true
That Mandeville delivers of his travels;   60
Yet I myself may be as well believ'd.
PEREGRINE.

Since you speak reverently of him, say on.
DOCTOR.

Of Europe I'll not speak; 'tis too near home:
Who's not familiar with the Spanish garb,
Th'Italian shrug, French cringe, and German hug?   65
Nor will I trouble you with my observations
Fetch'd from Arabia, Paphlagonia,
Mesopotamia, Mauritania,
Syria, Thessalia, Persia, India,
All still is too near home. Though I have touch'd   70
The clouds upon the Pyrenean mountains,
And been on Paphos Isle, where I have kiss'd
The image of bright Venus, all is still

64. *garb*] manner.
72. *Paphos Isle*] west coast of Cyprus, chief seat of worship of Aphrodite.

Too near home to be boasted.

DIANA [*aside*].

    That I like well in him, too; he will not   75
    Boast of kissing a woman too near home.

DOCTOR.

    These things in me
    Are poor; they sound in a far traveler's ear
    Like the reports of those that beggingly
    Have put out on returns from Edinburgh,   80
    Paris, or Venice, or perhaps Madrid,
    Whither a milliner may with half a nose
    Smell out his way, and is not near so difficult
    As for some man in debt, and unprotected,
    To walk from Charing Cross to th'old Exchange.   85
    No, I will pitch no nearer than th' Antipodes,
    That which is farthest distant, foot to foot
    Against our region.

DIANA.   What, with their heels upwards?

    Bless us! How scape they breaking o' their necks?

DOCTOR.

    They walk upon firm earth, as we do here,   90
    And have the firmament over their heads,
    As we have here.

DIANA.   And yet just under us!

    Where is hell then? If they whose feet are towards us,
    At the lower part of the world, have heaven, too,
    Beyond their heads, where's hell?

JOYLESS.   You may find that   95

    Without inquiry. Cease your idle questions.

DIANA.

    Sure hell's above ground, then, in jealous husbands.

PEREGRINE.

    What people, sir (I pray, proceed) what people
    Are they of the Antipodes? Are they not such

---

    82. *milliner*] originally a native of Milan; also a vendor of fancy wares or articles of apparel, especially of Milan manufacture.
    85. *old Exchange*] Royal Exchange, established by Gresham in 1567.
    86–87. *Antipodes . . . foot*] Cf. Mandeville, Chap. CIV (sig. T4), titled "How Prester John land lyeth foote againe foot to England."

As Mandeville writes of, without heads or necks,   100
Having their eyes plac'd on their shoulders, and
Their mouths amidst their breasts?

DIANA.   Ay so, indeed,
Though heels go upwards, and their feet should slip,
They have no necks to break.

DOCTOR.   Silence, sweet lady;
Pray give the gentleman leave to understand me.   105
The people through the whole world of Antipodes,
In outward feature, language, and religion,
Resemble those to whom they are supposite:
They under Spain appear like Spaniards;
Under France, Frenchmen; under England, English   110
To the exterior show; but in their manners,
Their carriage, and condition of life,
Extremely contrary. To come close to you,
What part o'th' world's Antipodes shall I now
Decipher to you, or would you travel to?   115

PEREGRINE.
The furthest off.

DOCTOR.   That is th' Antipodes of England.
The people there are contrary to us,
As thus: here (heaven be prais'd) the magistrates
Govern the people; there the people rule
The magistrates.

DIANA.   There's precious bribing then.   120

JOYLESS.
You'll hold your peace.

DOCTOR.   Nay, lady, 'tis by nature.
Here generally men govern the women—

JOYLESS.
I would they could else.

DIANA.   You will hold your peace!

100–102. *without . . . breasts*] Mandeville, Chap. LXII, sig. O2ᵛ.
108. *supposite*] "situated below" (*OED*), the only example given for this
meaning.

DOCTOR.
But there the women overrule the men.
If some men fail here in their power, some women   125
Slip their holds there. As parents here, and masters
Command, there they obey the child and servant.
DIANA.
But pray, sir, is't by nature or by art
That wives o'ersway their husbands there?
DOCTOR.   By nature.
DIANA.
Then art's above nature, as they are under us.   130
DOCTOR.
In brief, sir, all
Degrees of people, both in sex and quality,
Deport themselves in life and conversation
Quite contrary to us.
DIANA.   Why then, the women
Do get the men with child, and put the poor fools   135
To grievous pain, I warrant you, in bearing.
JOYLESS.
Into your chamber; get you in, I charge you.
DOCTOR.
By no means, as you tender your son's good.
No, lady, no; that were to make men women,
And women men. But there the maids do woo   140
The bachelors, and 'tis most probable,
The wives lie uppermost.
DIANA.   That is a trim,
Upside down, Antipodean trick indeed!
DOCTOR.
And then at christenings and gossips' feasts,
A woman is not seen: the men do all   145
The tittle-tattle duties, while the women
Hunt, hawk, and take their pleasure.
PEREGRINE.
Ha' they good game, I pray, sir?
DOCTOR.   Excellent;
But by the contraries to ours, for where
We hawk at pheasant, partridge, mallard, heron,   150

With goshawk, tercel, falcon, lanneret,
Our hawks become their game, our game their hawks.
And so the like in hunting: there the deer
Pursue the hounds; and (which you may think strange)
I ha' seen one sheep worry a dozen foxes   155
By moonshine in a morning before day.
They hunt train-scents with oxen, and plow with dogs.

PEREGRINE [*laughing*].   Hugh, hugh, hugh!

DIANA.
    Are not their swans all black, and ravens white?

DOCTOR.
    Yes, indeed are they, and their parrots teach
Their mistresses to talk.

DIANA.   That's very strange.   160

DOCTOR.
    They keep their cats in cages,
From mice that would devour them else; and birds
Teach 'em to whistle and cry "Beware the rats, Puss."
But these are frivolous nothings. I have known
Great ladies ride great horses, run at tilt,   165
At ring, races, and hunting matches, while
Their lords at home have painted, pawned their plate
And jewels to feast their honorable servants;
And there the merchants' wives do deal abroad
Beyond seas, while their husbands cuckold them   170
At home.

DIANA.   Then there are cuckolds, too, it seems,
As well as here.

JOYLESS.   Then you conclude here are!

---

151. *goshawk*] from old English "gos-hafoc," a large short-winged hawk used for hunting pheasants and rabbits, usually assigned to rank of yeoman (Strutt, p. 36).

151. *tercel*] in falconry, the male of any Peregrine falcon and goshawk, assigned to the rank of poor man (Strutt, p. 37).

151. *lanneret*] the male of lanner, a species of falcon found in countries bordering on the Mediterranean, assigned to the rank of an esquire (Strutt, p. 37); the diminutive title because the male, lanneret, is smaller than the female, lanner (Baker).

166. *At ring*] a sport in which a number of riders endeavor to carry off on the point of their lances a circlet of metal suspended from a post.

DIANA.
    By hearsay, sir; I am not wise enough
    To speak it on my knowledge yet.
JOYLESS.   Not yet!
DOCTOR.
    Patience, good sir.
PEREGRINE.   Hugh, hugh, hugh!   175
DOCTOR.
    What, do you laugh that there is cuckold-making
    In the Antipodes? I tell you, sir,
    It is not so abhorr'd here as 'tis held
    In reputation there: all your old men
    Do marry girls, and old women, boys,   180
    As generation were to be maintain'd
    Only by cuckold-making.
JOYLESS.   Monstrous!
DOCTOR.   Pray, your patience.
    There's no such honest men there in their world
    As are their lawyers: they give away
    Their practice, and t'enable 'em to do so,   185
    Being all handicrafts or laboring men,
    They work (poor hearts, full hard) in the vacations
    To give their law for nothing in the term times.
    No fees are taken, which makes their divines,
    Being generally covetous, the greatest wranglers,   190
    In lawsuits, of a kingdom. You have not there
    A gentleman in debt, though citizens
    Haunt them with cap in hand to take their wares
    On credit.
DIANA.   What fine sport would that be here now!
DOCTOR.
    All wit, and mirth, and good society   195
    Is there among the hirelings, clowns, and tradesmen;
    And all their poets are puritans.
DIANA.   Ha' they poets?

---

187. *vacations*] periods in the year when law courts are suspended.
188. *term times*] with reference to the legal terms: Hilary, Easter, Trinity, and Michaelmas.

DOCTOR.

    And players, too; but they are all the sob'rest,
    Precisest people pick'd out of a nation.

DIANA.

    I never saw a play.

DOCTOR.   Lady, you shall.

JOYLESS.   She shall not.   200

DOCTOR.

    She must, if you can hope for any cure.
    Be govern'd, sir; your jealousy will grow
    A worse disease than your son's madness else.
    You are content I take the course I told you of
    To cure the gentleman?

JOYLESS.   I must be, sir.   205

DOCTOR.

    Say, Master Peregrine, will you travel now
    With me to the Antipodes, or has not
    The journey wearied you in the description?

PEREGRINE.

    No, I could hear you a whole fortnight, but
    Let's lose no time; pray, talk on as we pass.   210

DOCTOR.

    First, sir, a health to auspicate our travels,
    And we'll away.

[I.vii]   *Enter* Blaze.

PEREGRINE.

    Gi'me't. What's he? One sent,
    I fear, from my dead mother to make stop
    Of our intended voyage.

DOCTOR.   No, sir; drink.

BLAZE [*aside to* Doctor].

    My lord, sir, understands the course y'are in
    By your letters, he tells me, and bade me gi' you   5
    This ring, which wants a finger here, he says.

PEREGRINE.

    We'll not be stay'd?

209–210.] *Q contains marginal S.D.:*
A Bowle/ on the table.

DOCTOR.   No, sir, he brings me word
  The mariner calls away; the wind and tide
  Are fair, and they are ready to weigh anchor,
  Hoist sails, and only stay for us. Pray drink, sir.   10
PEREGRINE.
  A health then to the willing winds and seas,
  And all that steer towards th' Antipodes.
JOYLESS.
  He has not drunk so deep a draught this twelvemonth.
DOCTOR.
  'Tis a deep draught indeed, and now 'tis down,
  And carries him down to the Antipodes!   15
  I mean but in a dream.
JOYLESS.   Alas, I fear.
  See, he begins to sink.
DOCTOR.   Trust to my skill.
  Pray take an arm, and see him in his cabin.
  Good lady, save my ring that's fallen there.
DIANA.
  In sooth, a marvelous neat and costly one!   20
BLAZE [*aside*].
  So, so, the ring has found a finger.
DOCTOR.
  Come, sir, aboard, aboard, aboard, aboard!
                      [*Exeunt all except* Blaze.]
BLAZE.
  To bed, to bed, to bed; I know your voyage,
  And my dear lord's dear plot. I understand
  Whose ring hath pass'd here by your slight of hand.   25
                          [*Exit* Blaze.]

[II.i]   [*Enter*] Letoy, Doctor.

LETOY.
  Tonight, sayest thou, my Hughball?
DOCTOR.   By all means,
  And if your play takes to my expectation,
  As I not doubt my potion works to yours,
  Your fancy and my cure shall be cried up

---

1. S.P. LETOY] *not in* Q.

Miraculous. Oh, y'are the lord of fancy.   5

LETOY.

    I'm not ambitious of that title, sir.
    No, the Letoys are of antiquity
    Ages before the fancies were begot,
    And shall beget still new to the world's end.
    But are you confident o' your potion, Doctor?   10
    Sleeps the young man?

DOCTOR.   Yes, and has slept these twelve hours,
    After a thousand mile an hour outright
    By sea and land, and shall awake anon
    In the Antipodes.

LETOY.   Well, sir, my actors
    Are all in readiness, and, I think, all perfect   15
    But one, that never will be perfect in a thing
    He studies: yet he makes such shifts extempore,
    (Knowing the purpose what he is to speak to)
    That he moves mirth in me 'bove all the rest.
    For I am none of those poetic furies,   20
    That threats the actor's life, in a whole play,
    That adds a syllable or takes away.
    If he can fribble through, and move delight
    In others, I am pleas'd.

DOCTOR.

    It is that mimic fellow which your lordship   25
    But lately entertain'd.

LETOY.   The same.

DOCTOR.

    He will be wondrous apt in my affair,
    For I must take occasion to interchange
    Discourse with him sometimes amidst their scenes,
    T'inform my patient, my mad young traveler,   30
    In diverse matters.

---

    5. *fancy*] imagination, aptitude for invention or design.
    8. *fancies*] i.e., "toy" is the old word for "whim," "fancy" the modern
(so Baker).
    12. *After*] at the rate of.
    23. *fribble*] falter or stammer out.
    26. *entertain'd*] took into service.

LETOY.

    Do; put him to't. I use't myself sometimes.

DOCTOR.

    I know it is your way.

LETOY.   Well, to the business.

    Hast wrought the jealous gentleman, old Joyless,

    To suffer his wife to see our comedy?   35

DOCTOR.

    She brings your ring, my lord, upon her finger,

    And he brings her in's hand. I have instructed her

    To spur his jealousy off o'the legs.

LETOY.

    And I will help her in't.

DOCTOR.   The young distracted

    Gentlewoman, too, that's sick of her virginity,   40

    Yet knows not what it is, and Blaze and's wife

    Shall all be your guests tonight, and not alone

    Spectators, but (as we will carry it) actors

    To fill your comic scenes with double mirth.

LETOY.

    Go fetch 'em then, while I prepare my actors.   *Exit* Doctor. 45

    Within there ho!

1 (*within*).

    This is my beard and hair.

2 (*within*).

    My lord appointed it for my part.

3 (*within*).

    No, this is for you; and this is yours, this gray one.

4 (*within*).

    Where be the foils and targets for the women?   50

1 (*within*).

    Here, can't you see?

LETOY.

    What a rude coil is there! But yet it pleases me.

1 (*within*).

    You must not wear that cloak and hat.

43. actors] *Baker;* Actor Q.

---

  50. *targets*] shields.

  52. *coil*] turmoil, confusion.

2 (*within*).

    Who told you so? I must

    In my first scene, and you must wear that robe.   55

LETOY.

    What a noise make those knaves! Come in, one of you.

[II.ii]   *Enter* Quailpipe, *3 actors, and* Byplay.

LETOY.

    Are you the first that answers to that name?

QUAILPIPE.

    My lord.

LETOY.   Why are not you ready yet?

QUAILPIPE.

    I am not to put on my shape before

    I have spoke the Prologue. And for that, my lord,

    I yet want something.   5

LETOY.

    What, I pray, with your grave formality?

QUAILPIPE.

    I want my beaver shoes and leather cap

    To speak the Prologue in, which were appointed

    By your lordship's own direction.

LETOY.   Well, sir, well:

    There they be for you; I must look to all.   10

QUAILPIPE.

    Certes, my lord, it is a most apt conceit,

    The comedy being the world turn'd upside down,

    That the presenter wear the capital beaver

    Upon his feet, and on his head shoe leather.

LETOY.

    Trouble not you your head with my conceit,   15

    But mind your part. Let me not see you act now

    In your scholastic way you brought to town wi' ye,

0.1.] *after l. 1 in Q.*

---

3. *shape*] make-up and costume for a particular part.

11. *conceit*] idea, conception.

13. *presenter*] speaker of the Prologue.

13. *capital beaver*] beaver hat for the head.

With seesaw sack-a-down, like a sawyer;
Nor in a comic scene play *Hercules Furens*,
Tearing your throat to split the audient's ears.   20
And you, sir, you had got a trick of late
Of holding out your bum in a set speech,
Your fingers fibulating on your breast
As if your buttons or your band-strings were
Helps to your memory. Let me see you in't   25
No more, I charge you. No, nor you, sir, in
That over-action of the legs I told you of,
Your singles and your doubles. Look you, thus—
Like one o'th' dancing masters o'the Bear Garden.
And when you have spoke, at end of every speech,   30
Not minding the reply, you turn you round
As tumblers do, when betwixt every feat
They gather wind by firking up their breeches.
I'll none of these absurdities in my house,
But words and action married so together   35
That shall strike harmony in the ears and eyes
Of the severest, if judicious, critics.

QUAILPIPE.
My lord, we are corrected.

---

18. *seesaw sack-a-down*] This would seem to refer to an old nursery rhyme: "See-saw, sacradown;/ Which is the way to London town?/ One foot up, and the other down,/ And that is the way to London town./ 1. 2. 3. 4. 5./ I caught a hare alive;/ 6. 7. 8. 9. 10./ I let him go again"/ (quoted in *Percy Society* [1841] IV, ccxx, "Nursery Rhymes and Games," 124).

19. *Hercules Furens*] the ranter; a tragedy of Seneca's, translated by Jasper Heywood into English (1561).

20. *audient's*] listener's.

23. *fibulating*] fiddling with one's buttons; performing the act of buttoning and unbottoning.

24. *band-strings*] white tasseled ties used in the sixteenth and seventeenth centuries for fastening an ornamental ruff or collar, making it fit close to the neck.

28. *singles*] a particular step in dancing; i.e., "two steps, closing both feet" (Playford, sig. A4^v).

28. *doubles*] "four steps forward or back closing both feet" (Playford, sig. A4^v).

29. *dancing masters*] The bears were trained at the Bear Garden (Parish Garden) to dance and entertain.

33. *firking up*] hoisting up suddenly.

LETOY.   Go, be ready—

                                   [*Exeunt* Quailpipe *and three actors.*]

[*To* Byplay.]   But you, sir, are incorrigible, and
Take license to yourself to add unto   40
Your parts your own free fancy, and sometimes
To alter or diminish what the writer
With care and skill compos'd; and when you are
To speak to your coactors in the scene,
You hold interlocutions with the audients—   45

BYPLAY.

That is a way, my lord, has bin allow'd
On elder stages to move mirth and laughter.

LETOY.

Yes, in the days of Tarlton and Kemp,
Before the stage was purg'd from barbarism,
And brought to the perfection it now shines with.   50
Then fools and jesters spent their wits, because
The poets were wise enough to save their own
For profitabler uses. Let that pass.
Tonight I'll give thee leave to try thy wit
In answering my doctor and his patient   55
He brings along with him to our Antipodes.

BYPLAY.

I heard of him, my lord. Blaze gave me light
Of the mad patient, and that he never saw
A play in's life. It will be possible
For him to think he is in the Antipodes   60
Indeed, when he is on the stage among us,
When't has been thought by some that have their wits
That all the players i'th' town were sunk past rising.

LETOY.

Leave that, sir, to th'event. See all be ready:

---

46. *bin*] dialectical form of "been" (*OED*).

48. *Tarlton*] famous sixteenth-century Elizabethan comedian and jester
to Queen Elizabeth; he was noted for his jigs and for his singing extemporaneous rhymes to the accompaniment of tabor and pipe.

48. *Kemp*] William Kemp, early seventeenth-century comic actor and
dancer who, soon after Tarlton died in 1588, succeeded to his roles and
reputation. Brome here alludes to his practice of interpolated buffoonery.

63. *sunk . . . rising*] another reference to the theater closure between May,
1636, and October, 1637, because of the plague.

    Your music, properties, and—

BYPLAY.   All, my lord,   65
    Only we want a person for a mute.

LETOY.
    Blaze when he comes shall serve. Go in.   *Exit* Byplay.
    My guests, I hear, are coming.

[II.iii]   *Enter* Blaze, Joyless, Diana, Martha, Barbara.

BLAZE.
    My lord, I am become your honor's usher
    To these your guests, the worthy Mr. Joyless,
    With his fair wife and daughter-in-law.

LETOY.   They're welcome,
    And you in the first place, sweet Mistress Joyless.
    You wear my ring, I see; you grace me in it.   5

JOYLESS.
    His ring! What ring? How came she by't?

BLAZE [*aside*].   'Twill work.

LETOY.
    I sent it as a pledge of my affection to you,
    For I before have seen you, and do languish
    Until I shall enjoy your love.

JOYLESS [*aside*].   He courts her.

LETOY.
    Next Lady—you—I have a toy for you, too.   10

MARTHA.
    My child shall thank you for it, when I have one.
    I take no joy in toys since I was married.

LETOY.
    Prettily answer'd—I make you no stranger,
    Kind Mistress Blaze.

BARBARA.   Time was your honor us'd
    Me strangely, too, as you'll do these, I doubt not.   15

LETOY.
    Honest Blaze,
    Prithee go in; there is an actor wanting.

---

   10. *toy*] trifle.
   15. *strangely*] in bawdy sense, to be sexually intimate with (so Partridge,
p. 214).

BLAZE.
    Is there a part for me? How shall I study't?
LETOY.
    Thou shalt say nothing.
BLAZE.   Then if I do not act
    Nothing as well as the best of 'em, let me be hiss'd.   *Exit.*   20
JOYLESS [*aside to* Diana].
    I say restore the ring, and back with me.
DIANA.
    To whom shall I restore it?
JOYLESS.   To the lord that sent it.
DIANA.
    Is he a lord? I always thought and heard
    I'th' country, lords were gallant creatures. He
    Looks like a thing not worth it. 'Tis not his;   25
    The doctor gave it me, and I will keep it.
LETOY.
    I use small verbal courtesy, Mr. Joyless,
    You see, but what I can in deed, I'll do.
    You know the purpose of your coming, and
    I can but give you welcome. If your son   30
    Shall receive ease in't, be the comfort yours,
    The credit of't my doctor's. You are sad.
JOYLESS.
    My lord, I would entreat we may return;
    I fear my wife's not well.
LETOY.
    Return! Pray, slight not so my courtesy.   35
DIANA.
    Besides, sir, I am well, and have a mind,
    A thankful one, to taste my lord's free bounty.
    I never saw a play, and would be loath
    To lose my longing now.
JOYLESS [*aside*].   The air of London
    Hath tainted her obedience already,   40
    And should the play but touch the vices of it,
    She'd learn and practice 'em. —Let me beseech
    Your lordship's reacceptance of the un-
    Merited favor that she wears here, and
    Your leave for our departure.

LETOY.   I will not   45
   Be so dishonored, nor become so ill
   A master of my house, to let a lady
   Leave it against her will, and from her longing.
   I will be plain wi' ye therefore; if your haste
   Must needs post you away, you may depart.   50
   She shall not till the morning, for mine honor.
JOYLESS.
   Indeed, 'tis a high point of honor in
   A lord to keep a private gentleman's wife
   From him.
DIANA.   I love this plain lord better than
   All the brave, gallant ones that e'er I dreamt on.   55
LETOY.
   'Tis time we take our seats. So if you'll stay,
   Come sit with us; if not, you know your way.
JOYLESS.
   Here are we fallen through the doctor's fingers
   Into the lord's hands. Fate, deliver us.   *Exeunt omnes.*

[II.iv]

Enter in sea gowns and caps, Doctor, *and* Peregrine *brought in a chair by two sailors. Cloaks and hats brought in.*

DOCTOR.
   Now the last minute of his sleeping fit
   Determines. Raise him on his feet. So, so:
   Rest him upon mine arm. Remove that chair. —
   Welcome ashore, sir, in th' Antipodes.
PEREGRINE.
   Are we arriv'd so far?
DOCTOR.   And on firm land.   5
   Sailors, you may return now to your ship.   *Exeunt sailors.*

51. not] *Baker;* not not *Q.*

---

   48. *from*] contrary to.
[II.iv]
   0.1. *sea gowns*] sailors' cloaks.
   0.1. *chair*] a bed-chair, a litter.
   2. *Determines*] ends.

PEREGRINE.

    What worlds of lands and seas have I pass'd over,
    Neglecting to set down my observations!
    A thousand thousand things remarkable
    Have slipp'd my memory, as if all had been   10
    Mere shadowy phantasms, or fantastic dreams.

DOCTOR.

    We'll write as we return, sir; and 'tis true,
    You slept most part o'th' journey hitherward,
    The air was so somniferous. And 'twas well;
    You scap'd the calenture by't.   15

PEREGRINE.

    But how long do you think I slept?

DOCTOR.

    Eight months, and some odd days,
    Which was but as so many hours and minutes
    Of one's own natural country sleep.

PEREGRINE.

    Eight months?—

DOCTOR.   'Twas nothing for so young a brain.   20
    How think you one of the seven Christian champions,
    David by name, slept seven years in a leek bed?

---

15. *calenture*] a burning fever incident to sailors within the tropics "characterized by delirium in which the patient, it is said, fancies the sea to be green fields, and desires to leap into it" (*OED*).

19. *country sleep*] common phrase for pregnancy, alluding to the practice of city women "visiting friends in the country" when they were pregnant.

21. *seven Christian champions*] Professor Baker records an old ballad beginning: "St. George, he was for England, St. Dennis was for France; St. James for Spain, whose valiant hand Did Christian Fame advance: St. Anthony for Italy; Andrew for Scots ne'er fails; Patrick, too, for Ireland; St. David was for Wales." The exploits of the saints are celebrated in many forms of literature, e.g., Richard Johnson's romance, *The Most Famous Historie of the Seaven Champions of Christendom* (edn. 1596): John Kirke's play, *The Seven Champions of Christendome* (edn. 1638), acted at the Cockpit and at the Red Bull, *c.* 1634–1638.

22–23. *David ... history*] According to Richard Johnson's *Famous Historie*, David is overcome by magic with a deep sleep. Four spirits in the likeness of beautiful damsels wrapped "the drowsie Champion in a sheet of the fine Arabian silke, and convayed him into a cave, directly placed in the middle of the Garden, where they layed him upon a soft bed, more softer then the downe of Culvers: where those beautifull ladies through the artes

PEREGRINE.

I think I have read it in their famous history.

DOCTOR.

But what chief thing of note now in our travels
Can you call presently to mind? Speak like a traveler.   25

PEREGRINE.

I do remember, as we pass'd the verge
O'th' upper world, coming down, downhill,
The setting sun, then bidding them good night,
Came gliding easily down by us and struck
New day before us, lighting us our way,   30
But with such heat that till he was got far
Before us, we even melted.

DOCTOR [*aside*].   Well-wrought potion!—
Very well observ'd, sir.
But now we are come into a temperate clime,
Of equal composition of elements   35
With that of London, and as well agreeable
Unto our nature as you have found that air.

PEREGRINE.

I never was at London.

DOCTOR.   Cry you mercy.
This, sir, is Anti-London. That's the Antipodes
To the grand city of our nation: 40
Just the same people, language, and religion,
But contrary in manners, as I ha' told you.

PEREGRINE.

I do remember that relation
As if you had but given it me this morning.

DOCTOR.

Now cast your sea weeds off, and don fresh garments.   45

45. don] *Baker;* do'n *Q.*

---

of Wicked *Ormondine,* continually kept him sleeping for the tearme of seaven
yeares: one while singing with sugred songes, more sweeter ..." (edn.
1596, Chap. IX, sig. M4). Brome, of course, enhances the soporific delights
of the Welch Knight by supplying him with a leek bed.
    34. *clime*] climate.
    38. *Cry you mercy*] Seeing that Peregrine has forgotten his recent coming to
London, the Doctor instantly resolves to humor him (Baker).
    40. *grand*] chief (Onions).

[*They*] *shift* [*their sea gowns and caps for the cloaks and hats*].
Heark, sir, their music.

[II.v]
Hoboys. Enter Letoy, Joyless, Diana, Martha, Barbara *in masks. They
sit at the other end of the stage.*

LETOY.
Here we may sit, and he not see us.
DOCTOR.
Now see one of the natives of this country.
Note his attire, his language, and behavior.

Enter Quailpipe [*as*] *Prologue.*
QUAILPIPE.
Our far fetch'd title over lands and seas
Offers unto your view th' Antipodes.   5
But what Antipodes now shall you see?
Even those that foot to foot 'gainst London be,
Because no traveler that knows that state
Shall say we personate or imitate
Them in our actions; for nothing can,   10
Almost, be spoke, but some or other man
Takes it unto himself and says the stuff,
If it be vicious or absurd enough,
Was woven upon his back. Far, far be all
That bring such prejudice mix'd with their gall.   15
This play shall no satiric timist be
To tax or touch at either him or thee
That art notorious. 'Tis so far below
Things in our orb that do among us flow,
That no degree, from kaiser to the clown,   20
Shall say this vice or folly was mine own.

45.1] *Q prints in margin at right of
l. 46.*

---

4. *title*] reference to the placard or "playboard" hung over the stage;
cf. Kyd's *Spanish Tragedy* (edn. 1592), IV.iii: "Hang up the Title; Our
scene is Rhodes" (*OED*).

16. *satiric timist*] one who follows the humor of the time (*OED*);
therefore satirist.

LETOY.

    This had bin well now, if you had not dreamt

    Too long upon your syllables.   *Exit* Prologue.

DIANA.

    The Prologue call you this, my lord?

BARBARA.

    'Tis my lord's reader, and as good a lad   25

    Out of his function as I would desire

    To mix withall in civil conversation.

LETOY.

    Yes, Lady, this was prologue to the play,

    As this is to our sweet ensuing pleasures.   *Kiss.*

JOYLESS.

    Kissing indeed is prologue to a play,   30

    Compos'd by th' devil, and acted by the Children

    Of his Black Revels; may hell take ye for't.

MARTHA.

    Indeed I am weary, and would fain go home.

BARBARA.

    Indeed but you must stay, and see the play.

MARTHA.

    The play? What play? It is no children's play, 35

    Nor no child-getting play, pray, is it?

BARBARA.

    You'll see anon. Oh, now the actors enter.   *Flourish.*

[II.vi]

Enter two Sergeants, *with swords drawn, running before a* Gentleman.

---

22. *dreamt*] drawled out.

25. *reader*] an allusion to the careless observance of the forms of religion, whereby laymen of questionable repute or a "neighbor's son that had been awhile at school" were employed as readers in chapels and churches lacking a clergy (*The Practical Works of the Rev. Richard Baxter*, edn. 1830, V, 538).

31–32. *Children . . . Revels*] a pun: (1) Children of the Revels; (2) their theater, Blackfriars. Brome wrote for the Children of the King's Revels during the first year or so of his contract with Salisbury Court.

[II.vi]

0.1. *Sergeants*] an officer whose duty it was to arrest offenders or to summon persons to appear before court.

GENTLEMAN.

    Why do you not your office, courteous friends?
    Let me entreat you stay, and take me with you.
    Lay but your hands on me; I shall not rest
    Until I be arrested. A sore shoulder ache
    Pains and torments me till your virtuous hands   5
    Do clap or stroke it.

1 SERGEANT.   You shall pardon us.

2 SERGEANT.

    And I beseech you pardon our intent,
    Which was indeed to have arrested you;
    But sooner shall the charter of the city
    Be forfeited than varlets like ourselves   10
    Shall wrong a gentleman's peace. So fare you well, sir.

                            Exeunt [Sergeants].

GENTLEMAN.

    Oh, y'are unkind.

PEREGRINE.   Pray, what are those?

DOCTOR.   Two catchpoles

    Run from a gentleman, it seems, that would
    Have bin arrested.

[II.vii]   *Enter old* Lady *and* Byplay, *like a servingman.*

LADY.

    Yonder's your master.
    Go, take him you in hand, while I fetch breath.

BYPLAY.

    Oh, are you here? My lady and myself
    Have sought you sweetly.

LETOY.   You and your lady, you

    Should ha' said, Puppy.

BYPLAY.   For we heard you were   5

    To be arrested. Pray, sir, who has bail'd you?
    I wonder who of all your bold acquaintance
    That knows my lady durst bail off her husband.

---

    4. *shoulder ache*] pitchfork-like instruments with barbed springs at the side were used by sergeants or *catchpoles* (l. 12).
[II.vii]
    4. *sweetly*] said ironically (Baker).

GENTLEMAN.
　　Indeed, I was not touch'd.
BYPLAY.　　　　　　　　　Have you not made
　　An end by composition, and disburs'd　　　　　　　10
　　Some of my lady's money for a peace
　　That shall beget an open war upon you?
　　Confess it if you have, for 'twill come out.
　　She'll ha' you up, you know. I speak it for your good.
GENTLEMAN.
　　I know't, and I'll entreat my lady wife　　　　　　15
　　To mend thy wages tother forty shillings
　　A year for thy true care of me.
LADY.　　　　　　　　　　　'Tis well, sir.
　　But now (if thou hast impudence so much
　　As face to face to speak unto a lady
　　That is thy wife and supreme head) tell me　　　　　20
　　At whose suit was it? or upon what action?
　　Debts I presume you have none, for who dares trust
　　A lady's husband who is but a squire
　　And under covert-barne? It is some trespass—
　　Answer me not till I find out the truth.　　　　　　25
GENTLEMAN.
　　The truth is—
LADY.　　　　　　Peace!
　　How darst thou speak the truth
　　Before thy wife! I'll find it out myself.
DIANA.
　　In truth, she handles him handsomely.
JOYLESS.　　　　　　　　　　Do you like it?
DIANA.
　　Yes, and such wives are worthy to be like'd　　　　30
　　For giving good example.
LETOY.　　　　　　　Good! Hold up
　　That humor by all means.
LADY.　　　　　　　　I think I ha' found it.

　　10. *composition*] an agreement.
　　24. *covert-barne*] corruption of "covert-baron." The term is used of a wife because she is "under the protection and influence of her husband, her *baron*, or lord" (*OED*).

There was a certain mercer sent you silks,
And cloth of gold to get his wife with child;
You slighted her, and answered not his hopes,   35
And now he lays to arrest you. Is't not so?

GENTLEMAN.

Indeed, my lady wife, 'tis so.

LADY.   For shame!
Be not ingrateful to that honest man,
To take his wares and scorn to lie with his wife.
Do't, I command you. What did I marry you for?   40
The portion that you brought me was not so
Abundant, though it were five thousand pounds
(Considering, too, the jointure that I made you),
That you should disobey me.

DIANA.   It seems the husbands
In the Antipodes bring portions, and   45
The wives make jointures.

JOYLESS.   Very well observ'd.

DIANA.

And wives, when they are old and past childbearing,
Allow their youthful husbands other women.

LETOY.

Right. And old men give their young wives like license.

DIANA.

That I like well. Why should not our old men   50
Love their young wives as well?

JOYLESS.   Would you have it so?

LETOY.

Peace, Master Joyless, you are too loud. Good still.

BYPLAY.

Do as my lady bids. You got her woman
With child at half these words.

GENTLEMAN.   Oh, but another's
Wife is another thing. Far be it from   55
A gentleman's thought to do so, having a wife
And handmaid of his own that he loves better.

---

36. *lays*] makes arrangements or plans.
38. *ingrateful*] ungrateful.

BYPLAY.

There said you well, but take heed, I advise you,
How you love your own wench or your own wife
Better than other men's.
DIANA.   Good Antipodean counsel.   60
LADY.

Go to that woman; if she prove with child,
I'll take it as mine own.
GENTLEMAN.   Her husband would
Do so, but from my house I may not stray.
MARTHA.

If it be me your wife commends you to,
You shall not need to stray from your own house.   65
I'll go home with you.
BARBARA.   Precious! What do you mean?
Pray keep your seat; you'll put the players out.
JOYLESS.

Here's goodly stuff! She's in the Antipodes, too.
PEREGRINE [*seeing* Letoy *and guests*].   And what are those?
DOCTOR.   All Antipodeans.
Attend, good sir.
LADY.   You know your charge; obey it.   70

[II.viii]   *Enter* Waiting Woman, *great-bellied.*

WOMAN.

What is his charge? Or whom must he obey,
Good madam, with your wild authority?
You are his wife, 'tis true, and therein may,
According to our law, rule and control him.
But you must know withal, I am your servant   5
And bound by the same law to govern you
And be a stay to you in declining age,
To curb and qualify your headstrong will,
Which otherwise would ruin you. Moreover,

---

66. *Precious!*] an exclamation for *Precious blood* or *body*, usually used as
"God's precious" (*OED*).
[II.viii]
7. *stay*] support; also, control.

Though y'are his wife, I am a breeding mother   10
Of a dear child of his, and therein claim
More honor from him than you ought to challenge.

LADY.

Insooth, she speaks but reason.

GENTLEMAN.   Pray, let's home then.

WOMAN.

You have something there to look to, one would think,
If you had any care. How well you saw   15
Your father at school today! And knowing how apt
He is to play the truant.

GENTLEMAN.   But is he not

Yet gone to school?

WOMAN.   Stand by, and you shall see.

[II.ix]   *Enter three* Old Men *with satchels, &c.*

ALL 3.

Domine, domine duster.
Three knaves in a cluster, &c.

GENTLEMAN.

Oh, this is gallant pastime! Nay, come on,
Is this your school? Was that your lesson, ha?

1 OLD MAN.

Pray now, good son, indeed, indeed.

GENTLEMAN.   Indeed,   5
You shall to school. Away with him, and take
Their wagships with him, the whole cluster of 'em.

2 OLD MAN.

You shan't send us now, so you shan't.

3 OLD MAN.

We be none of your father, so we bean't.

GENTLEMAN.

Away with 'em, I say; and tell their schoolmistress   10

---

1. *Domine*] vocative case of "Dominus," meaning Lord or Master.
1–2. *Domine . . . &c*] another antipodal practice, i.e., old men behaving
like young school children.
8, 9. *shan't, bean't*] Midland dialect, but Brome more likely is suggesting
a child's talk.

What truants they are, and bid her pay 'em soundly.
ALL 3.
Oh, oh, oh.
BYPLAY.   Come, come, ye gallows-clappers.
DIANA.
Alas, will nobody beg pardon for
The poor old boys?
DOCTOR.   Sir, gentle sir, a word with you.
BYPLAY.
To strangers, sir, I can be gentle.
LETOY.   Good!   15
Now mark that fellow; he speaks extempore.
DIANA.
Extempore call you him? He's a dogged fellow
To the three poor old things there; fie upon him.
PEREGRINE.
Do men of such fair years here go to school?
BYPLAY.
They would die dunces else.   20
PEREGRINE.
Have you no young men scholars, sir, I pray,
When we have beardless doctors?
DOCTOR [aside].   He has wip'd my lips—
You question very wisely, sir.
BYPLAY.
So, sir, have we, and many reverend teachers,
Grave counselors at law, perfect statesmen,   25
That never knew use of razor, which may live
For want of wit to lose their offices.
These were great scholars in their youth. But when
Age grows upon men here, their learning wastes,
And so decays that if they live until   30

---

11. *pay 'em soundly*] customary practice among schoolmasters (here, schoolmistresses). Cf. *Compleat*, p. 27, where Peacham tells of a schoolmaster who during winter months "would ordinarily in a cold morning, whip his Boyes over for no other purpose then to get himselfe a heat."
12. *gallows-clappers*] gallows-bird or one who has been hanged, his body swaying like the clapper of a bell (*OED*).
22. *wip'd my lips*] i.e., has gotten the better of me.

Threescore, their sons send them to school again.
They'd die as speechless else as newborn children.

PEREGRINE.

'Tis a wise nation; and the piety
Of the young men most rare and commendable.
Yet give me, as a stranger, leave to beg   35
Their liberty this day; and what they lose by't,
My father, when he goes to school, shall answer.

JOYLESS.

I am abus'd on that side, too.

BYPLAY.   'Tis granted.
Hold up your heads and thank the gentleman,
Like scholars, with your heels now.   40

ALL 3.

Gratias, Gratias, Gratias—   *Exeunt.*

DIANA.

Well done, son Peregrine; he's in's wits, I hope.

JOYLESS.

If you lose yours the while, where's my advantage?

DIANA.

And trust me, 'twas well done, too, of Extempore
To let the poor old children loose. And now   45
I look well on him, he's a proper man.

JOYLESS.

She'll fall in love with the actor, and undo me.

DIANA.

Does not his lady love him, sweet my lord?

LETOY.

Love? Yes, and lie with him as her husband does
With's maid. It is their law in the Antipodes.   50

DIANA.

But we have no such laws with us.

JOYLESS.

Do you approve of such a law?

DIANA.   No, not so much
In this case, where the man and wife do lie

41. S.D.] *Baker; Exit. Q.*

---

33. *piety*] dutifulness.
46. *proper*] handsome.

With their inferior servants; but in the other,
Where the old citizen would arrest the gallant   55
That took his wares and would not lie with's wife,
There it seems reasonable, very reasonable.

JOYLESS.   Does it?

DIANA.

Make't your own case: you are an old man;
I love a gentleman; you give him rich presents
To get me a child (because you cannot). Must not   60
We look to have our bargain?

JOYLESS.   Give me leave
Now to be gone, my lord, though I leave her
Behind me; she is mad and not my wife,
And I may leave her.

LETOY.   Come, you are mov'd, I see.
I'll settle all, but first prevail with you   65
To taste my wine and sweetmeats. The comedians
Shall pause the while. This you must not deny me.

                    Exit [Letoy *with* Martha, Diana, *and* Barbara].

JOYLESS.

I must not live here always; that's my comfort.   *Exit.*

PEREGRINE.

I thank you, sir, for the poor men's release.
It was the first request that I have made   70
Since I came in these confines.

BYPLAY.   'Tis our custom
To deny strangers nothing: yea, to offer
Of anything we have that may be useful,
In courtesy to strangers. Will you therefore
Be pleas'd to enter, sir, this habitation,   75
And take such viands, beverage, and repose
As may refresh you after tedious travels?

DOCTOR.

Thou tak'st him right, for I am sure he's hungry.

PEREGRINE.

All I have seen since my arrival are
Wonders, but your humanity excels.   80

77. travels] *this edn.;* travailes *Q.*

80. *humanity*] courtesy.

BYPLAY.

    Virtue in the Antipodes only dwells.   [*Exeunt.*]

[III.i]   [*Enter*] Letoy, Joyless, Diana, Martha, Barbara.

LETOY.

    Yet, Mr. Joyless, are you pleas'd? You see
    Here's nothing but fair play, and all above board.

JOYLESS.

    But it is late, and these long intermissions
    By banqueting and courtship twixt the acts
    Will keep back the catastrophe of your play   5
    Until the morning light.

LETOY.   All shall be short.

JOYLESS.

    And then in midst of scenes
    You interrupt your actors, and tie them
    To lengthen time in silence, while you hold
    Discourse by th' by.

LETOY.   Pox o' thy jealousy.   10
    Because I give thy wife a look, or word
    Sometimes! What if I kiss (thus); I'll not eat her.

JOYLESS.

    So, so, his banquet works with him.

LETOY.

    And for my actors, they shall speak or not speak
    As much, or more, or less, and when I please.   15
    It is my way of pleasure, and I'll use it.
    So sit. They enter.   *Flourish.*

[III.ii]   *Enter* Lawyer *and* Poet.

LAWYER.

    Your case is clear; I understand it fully,
    And need no more instructions. This shall serve
    To firk your adversary from court to court.

---

    8. *tie*] prevent from speaking.
    9–10. *hold . . . by th' by*] talk aside (Baker).
    13. *banquet*] course of sweetmeats, fruit, and wine.
[III.ii]
    3. *firk*] drive.

If he stand out upon rebellious legs
But till *Octavus Michaelis* next,   5
I'll bring him on submissive knees.

DIANA.   What's he?

LETOY.

A lawyer, and his client there, a poet.

DIANA.

Goes law so torn, and poetry so brave?

JOYLESS.

Will you but give the actors leave to speak,
They may have done the sooner!

LAWYER.   Let me see;   10
This is your bill of parcels?

POET.   Yes, of all
My several wares, according to the rates
Delivered unto my debtor.

DIANA.   Wares, does he say?

LETOY.

Yes, poetry is good ware
In the Antipodes, though there be some ill payers,   15
As well as here; but law there rights the poets.

LAWYER.

Delivered, too; and for the use of The Right Worshipful
Mr. Alderman Humblebee, as followeth: *Imprimis*—   *Reads.*
Umh, I cannot read your hand; your character
Is bad, and your orthography much worse.   20
Read it yourself, pray.

DIANA.   Do aldermen
Love poetry in Antipodean London?

LETOY.

Better than ours do custard; but the worst

5. *Octavus*] *Baker; Octabis Q.*   22. Antipodean] *Baker;* Antipodea
7. there, a poet] *Q (corr.)*; there's a   *Q.*
Poet *Q (uncorr.).*

5. *Octavus Michaelis*] October 7, i.e., eight days (the octave) after
Michaelmas Day, September 29; one of the times for returning writs.
   11. *parcels*] an itemized account of charges for services rendered.
   19. *character*] handwriting.
   23. *custard*] "An immense custard was a conspicuous part of a city feast
in Brome's time. When the City kept a fool, it was customary for him, at
public entertainments, to leap into a bowl of custard set for the purpose"
(Gifford's *Jonson*, quoted in Baker).

Paymasters living there, worse than our gallants,
Partly for want of money, partly wit.   25

DIANA.
Can aldermen want wit and money, too?
That's wonderful.

POET.   *Imprimis*, sir, here is
For three religious madrigals to be sung
By th' holy vestals in Bridewell for the
Conversion of our city wives and daughters,   30
Ten groats apiece: it was his own agreement.

LAWYER.
'Tis very reasonable.

POET.   Item, twelve hymns
For the twelve sessions during his shrievalty,
Sung by the quire of Newgate in the praise
Of city clemency (for in that year   35
No guiltless person suffer'd by their judgment)
Ten groats apiece also.

LAWYER.   So, now it rises.

DIANA.
Why speaks your poet so demurely?

LETOY.   Oh,
'Tis a precise tone he has got among
The sober sisterhood.

DIANA.   Oh, I remember: 40
The doctor said poets were all puritans
In the Antipodes. But where's the doctor?
And where's your son, my Joyless?

LETOY.   Do not mind him.

---

29. *holy . . . Bridewell*] another example of Brome's antipodean thoroughness, i.e., his associating vestal virgins vowed to chastity with Bridewell, a
prison near Fleet Ditch and Blackfriars turned into a house of correction for
rogues and loose women.

31. *groats*] originally a groat was fourpence, but later groats had greater
value; generally considered as any small sum.

33. *shrievalty*] a sheriff's term of office.

34. *quire*] canters or beggars who, having resided at Newgate or another
prison, returned, when out, to their old trade of begging.

34. *Newgate*] a prison for felons and law-breakers.

39. *precise*] puritanical.

'Gainst a commander.
LAWYER.   Very easily thus:
The coachman's poor, and scarce his twelvemonths' wages,
Though't be five marks a year, will satisfy.
CAPTAIN.
Pray name no sum in marks; I have had too many   45
Of's marks already.
LAWYER.   So you owe the other
A debt of twenty pound, the coachman now
Shall for your satisfaction beat you out
Of debt.
CAPTAIN.   Beat me again?
LAWYER.   No, sir, he shall beat
For you your featherman, till he take his money.   50
CAPTAIN.
So I'll be satisfied, and help him to
More customers of my rank.
LAWYER.   Leave it to me then;
It shall be my posterity repeaten
That soldiers ought not to be dun'd or beaten.
Away and keep your money.
CAPTAIN.   Thank you, sir.   [*Exit.*] 55
DIANA.
An honest lawyer still! How he considers
The weak estate of a young gentleman
At arms. —But who comes here? a woman?

[III.iv]   *Enter* Buff Woman.

LETOY.
Yes, that has taken up the newest fashion
Of the town militasters.
DIANA.   Is it buff,
Or calfskin, trow? She looks as she could beat

III.iv.0.1.] *Q prints scene division*   *III.iii.56–58.*
and S.D. in margin at right of
_____

44. *marks*] a mark is 13*s*. 4*d*., or 2/3 of a pound sterling (*OED*).
46. *So*] to the extent.
[III.iv]
0.1. *Buff*] dressed in buff jerkin.
2. *militasters*] a soldier without military skill or knowledge.
3. *trow*] cf. I.iv.20, n.

Out a whole tavern garrison before her
Of mill tasters, call you 'em? If her husband   5
Be an old, jealous man, now, and can please her

                                        Lawyer *reads on papers.*

No better than most ancient husbands can,
I warrant she makes herself good upon him.

JOYLESS.

'Tis very good; the play begins to please me.

BUFF WOMAN [*to* Lawyer].

I wait to speak w' ye, sir, but must I stand   10
Your const'ring and piercing of your scribblings.

LAWYER.   Cry mercy, lady.

DIANA.

"Lady" does he call her?

LAWYER.

Thus far I have proceeded in your cause
I'th' marshal's court.

BUFF WOMAN.   But shall I have the combat?

LAWYER.

Pray, observe   15
The passages of my proceedings, and
The pro's and contra's in the windings, workings,
And carriage of the cause.

BUFF WOMAN.   Fah on your passages,
Your windy workings, and your fizzlings at
The bar. Come me to th' point. Is it decreed   20
A combat?

LAWYER.   Well, it is; and here's your order.

BUFF WOMAN.

Now thou hast spoken like a lawyer,
And here's thy fee.

LAWYER.   By no means, gentle lady.

BUFF WOMAN.

Take it, or I will beat thy carcass thinner
Than thou hast worn thy gown here.

---

11. *const'ring and piercing*] construing and parsing.

14. *marshal's court*] "A court which had jurisdiction of causes to which
domestic servants were parties; held by the steward of the king's household"
(Bouvier, *Law Dict.*, quoted by Baker).

LAWYER.   Pardon me.   25

BUFF WOMAN.
    Must I then take you in hand?

LAWYER.   Hold, hold; I take it.
                                                      [*Withdraws.*]

DIANA.
    Alas, poor man! He will take money yet
    Rather than blows; and so far he agrees
    With our rich lawyers, that sometimes give blows,
    And shrewd ones, for their money.

BUFF WOMAN.   Now victory   30
    Afford me, Fate, or bravely let me die.   *Exit.*

LETOY.
    Very well acted, that.

DIANA.   Goes she to fight now?

LETOY.
    You shall see that anon—

[III.v]   *Enter a* Beggar *and a* Gallant.

DIANA.
    What's here, what's here?
    A courtier, or some gallant, practicing
    The beggar's trade, who teaches him, I think.

LETOY.
    Y'are something near the subject.

BEGGAR.   Sir, excuse me; I have
    From time to time supplied you, without hope   5
    Or purpose to receive least retribution
    From you: no, not so much as thanks or bare
    Acknowledgment of the free benefits
    I have conferr'd upon you.

GALLANT.   Yet, good uncle.

BEGGAR.
    Yet do you now, when that my present store   10
    Responds not my occasions, seek to oppress me
    With vain petitionary breath for what I may not
    Give without fear of dangerous detriment?

---

11. *Responds not*] does not correspond to.

DIANA.

    In what a phrase the ragged orator
    Displays himself!

LETOY.   The beggars are the   15
    Most absolute courtiers in th' Antipodes.

GALLANT.

    If not a piece, yet spare me half a piece
    For goodness sake, good sir; did you but know
    My instant want, and to what virtuous use
    I would distribute it, I know you would not   20
    Hold back your charity.

DIANA.   And how feelingly
    He begs. Then as the beggars are the best
    Courtiers, it seems the courtiers are best beggars
    In the Antipodes; how contrary in all
    Are they to us!

BEGGAR.   Pray to what virtuous uses   25
    Would you put money to now, if you had it?

GALLANT.

    I would bestow a crown in ballads,
    Love pamphlets, and such poetical rarities
    To send down to my lady grandmother.
    She's very old, you know, and given much   30
    To contemplation; I know she'll send me for 'em,
    In puddings, bacon, souse, and pot-butter
    Enough to keep my chamber all this winter.
    So shall I save my father's whole allowance
    To lay upon my back, and not be forc'd   35
    To shift out from my study for my victuals.

DIANA.

    Belike he is some student.

BEGGAR.   There's a crown.

GALLANT.

    I would bestow another crown in
    Hobbyhorses and rattles for my grandfather,
    Whose legs and hearing fail him very much.   40

---

27. *crown*] five shillings.
32. *souse*] pickled feet or ears of pig or some other animal.
32. *pot-butter*] salted butter put up in pots.

Then, to preserve his sight, a Jack-a-lent
In a green sars'net suit; he'll make my father
To send me one of scarlet, or he'll cry
His eyes out for't.
DIANA.   Oh politic young student.
BEGGAR.
I have but just a fee left for my lawyer;   45
If he exact not that, I'll give it thee.
DIANA.
He'll take no fee (that's sure enough, young man)
Of beggars, I know that.
LETOY.   You are deceiv'd.
DIANA.
I'll speak to him myself, else, to remit it.
JOYLESS.
You will not, sure; will you turn actor, too?   50
Pray do, be put in for a share amongst 'em!
DIANA.
How must I be put in?
JOYLESS.   The players will quickly
Show you, if you perform your part; perhaps
They may want one to act the whore amongst 'em.
LETOY.
Fie, Master Joyless, y'are too foul.
JOYLESS.   My lord,   55
She is too fair, it seems, in your opinion,
For me; therefore, if you can find it lawful,
Keep her; I will be gone.
LETOY.   Now I protest
Sit, and sit civilly, till the play be done;
I'll lock thee up else, as I am true Letoy.   60
JOYLESS.
Nay, I ha' done.   *Whistles "Fortune My Foe."*

---

41. *Jack-a-lent*] puppets set up to be pelted during Lent.
42. *sars'net*] a fine, soft silk material.
51. *put . . . share*] It was common for principal actors to be shareholders
in a theatrical company.
61.S.D. *Fortune My Foe*] the popular "hanging tune," long identified with
mourning and doleful matters.

LAWYER.
   Give me my fee; I cannot hear you else.
BEGGAR.
   Sir, I am poor, and all I get is at
   The hands of charitable givers; pray, sir—
LAWYER.
   You understand me, sir: your cause is to be   65
   Pleaded today, or you are quite o'erthrown in't.
   The judge by this time is about to sit.
   Keep fast your money, and forgo your wit.   *Exit.*
BEGGAR.
   Then I must follow, and entreat him to it;
   Poor men in law must not disdain to do it.   *Exit.* 70
GALLANT.
   Do it then; I'll follow you and hear the cause.   *Exit.*
DIANA.
   True Antipodeans still; for as with us,
   The gallants follow lawyers, and the beggars them,
   The lawyer here is follow'd by the beggar,
   While the gentleman follows him.   75
LETOY.
   The moral is, the lawyers here prove beggars,
   And beggars only thrive by going to law.
DIANA.
   How takes the lawyers, then, the beggars' money,
   And none else by their wills?
LETOY.   They send it all
   Up to our lawyers, to stop their mouths   80
   That curse poor clients that are put upon 'em
   In forma pauperis.
DIANA.   In truth most charitable,
   But sure that money's lost by th' way sometimes.
   Yet, sweet my lord, whom do these beggars beg of,
   That they can get aforehand so for law?   85
   Who are their benefactors?
LETOY.   Usurers, usurers.
DIANA.
   Then they have usurers in th' Antipodes, too?

82. *In forma pauperis*] the practice in law allowing the poor to sue or
defend in a court of law without paying costs.

LETOY.

    Yes, usury goes round the world, and will do,
    Till the general conversion of the Jews.

DIANA.

    But ours are not so charitable, I fear.   90
    Who be their usurers?

LETOY.   Soldiers and courtiers chiefly,
    And some that pass for grave and pious churchmen.

DIANA.

    How finely contrary th'are still to ours.

[III.vi]

LETOY.

    Why do you not enter? What, are you asleep?

Enter Byplay.

BYPLAY.

    My lord, the mad young gentleman—

JOYLESS.   What of him?

BYPLAY.

    He has got into our tiring house amongst us,
    And ta'en a strict survey of all our properties:
    Our statues and our images of gods, our planets and our
        constellations,   5
    Our giants, monsters, furies, beasts, and bugbears,
    Our helmets, shields, and vizors, hairs, and beards,
    Our pasteboard marchpanes, and our wooden pies.

LETOY.

    Sirrah, be brief; be not you now as long in

III.vi] *Misnumbered* Scene. 5. *in Q.*   1.1.] *above l. 1 in Q.*

---

    3. *tiring house*] dressing room; also used for storage.
    4–31. *properties . . . conquest*] Apprentices were in the habit of attacking and demolishing houses of ill fame on Shrove Tuesday; here one is reminded of the notorious Shrove Tuesday attack, March 4, 1617, celebrated in "A Ballad in praise of London Prentices, and what they did at the Cockpit Play-house, in Drury Lane" (in *Percy Society*, I [1841], 94–97). After listing the costumes, properties, and playhouse books destroyed, the ballad ends on the same note of puritanical self-righteousness evident in Peregrine's exploit.
    7. *vizors*] masks.
    8. *marchpanes*] confectionery made of almond paste, sugar, etc., often cast from elaborate molds and gilded for banqueting dishes.

Telling what he saw as he surveying.   10
BYPLAY.
    Whether he thought 'twas some enchanted castle,
    Or temple, hung and pil'd with monuments
    Of uncouth and of various aspects,
    I dive not to his thoughts. Wonder he did
    A while it seem'd, but yet undaunted stood;   15
    When on the sudden, with thrice knightly force,
    And thrice, thrice puissant arm he snatcheth down
    The sword and shield that I play'd Bevis with,
    Rusheth amongst the foresaid properties,
    Kills monster after monster, takes the puppets   20
    Prisoners, knocks down the Cyclops, tumbles all
    Our jigambobs and trinkets to the wall.
    Spying at last the crown and royal robes
    I'th' upper wardrobe, next to which by chance
    The devil's vizors hung, and their flame-painted   25
    Skin coats, those he remov'd with greater fury,
    And (having cut the infernal ugly faces
    All into mammocks) with a reverend hand,
    He takes the imperial diadem and crowns
    Himself King of the Antipodes, and believes   30
    He has justly gain'd the kingdom by his conquest.
LETOY.
    Let him enjoy his fancy.
BYPLAY.   Doctor Hughball
    Hath sooth'd him in't, so that nothing can
    Be said against it. He begins to govern
    With purpose to reduce the manners   35
    Of this country to his own. H' has constituted
    The doctor his chief officer, whose secretary
    I am to be; you'll see a court well ordered.
LETOY.
    I see th'event already, by the aim

---

    12. *monuments*] carved figures or effigies.
    18. *Bevis*] Sir Bevis of Hampton, i.e., Earl of Southampton, the hero of a popular medieval romance.
    22. *jigambobs*] variation of jiggumbob; anything odd or fanciful, a knickknack (*OED*).
    28. *mammocks*] shreds, small pieces.

The doctor takes. Proceed you with your play,   40
And let him see it in what state he pleases.

BYPLAY.
    I go, my lord.   *Exit.*

            Letoy *whispers with* Barbara.

DIANA.   Trust me, this same Extempore
    (I know not's tother name) pleases me better
    For absolute action than all the rest.

JOYLESS.
    You were best beg him of his lord.

DIANA.   Say you so?   45
    He's busy, or I'd move him.

LETOY.   Prithee do so,
    Good Mistress Blaze.—(*To* Martha.) Go with her, gentle
      lady.
    Do as she bids you. You shall get a child by't.

MARTHA.
    I'll do as anybody bids me for a child.

JOYLESS.
    Diana, yet be wise; bear not the name   50
    Of sober chastity to play the beast in.

DIANA.
    Think not yourself, nor make yourself a beast
    Before you are one; and when you appear so,
    Then thank yourself. Your jealousy durst not trust me
    Behind you in the country, and since I'm here,   55
    I'll see and know and follow th' fashion; if
    It be to cuckold you, I cannot help it.

JOYLESS.
    I now could wish my son had been as far
    In the Antipodes as he thinks himself,
    Ere I had run this hazard.

LETOY [*to* Barbara].   Y'are instructed.   60

BARBARA.
    And I'll perform't, I warrant you, my lord.
                Exeunt Barbara, Martha.

42. S.D.] Q *prints in margin at right*
of ll. 39–40.

DIANA.

    Why should you wish so? Had you rather lose
    Your son than please your wife? You show your love both ways.

LETOY.

    Now what's the matter?

JOYLESS.   Nothing, nothing.

LETOY.   Sit,

    The actors enter.   *Flourish.* 65

[III.vii]

Enter Byplay [*as*] *the governor, macebearer,* Swordbearer, Officer; *the mace and sword laid on the table. The governor sits.*

DIANA.

    What's he, a king?

LETOY.   No, 'tis the city governor,
    And the chief judge within their corporation.

JOYLESS.

    Here's a city

                 Enter Peregrine *and* Doctor.

    Like to be well govern'd then.

LETOY.

    Yonder's a king. Do you know him?

DIANA.   'Tis your son,   5
    My Joyless; now y'are pleas'd.

JOYLESS.   Would you were pleas'd
    To cease your huswif'ry in spinning out
    The play at length thus.

DOCTOR.   Here, sir, you shall see
    A point of justice handled.

BYPLAY.   Officer.

OFFICER.   My lord.

BYPLAY.

    Call the defendant and the plaintiff in.   10

SWORDBEARER.

    Their counsel and their witnesses.

BYPLAY.   How now!

III.vii] *Misnumbered* Scene 6. *in* Q.

Example to the breach of city custom,
By gentlemen's neglect of tradesmen's wives)—   60
I should say for this contempt commit you
Prisoner from sight of any other woman
Until you give this man's wife satisfaction,
And she release you; justice so would have it.
But as I am a citizen by nature   65
(For education made it so), I'll use
Urbanity in your behalf towards you;
And as I am a gentleman by calling
(For so my place must have it), I'll perform
For you the office of a gentleman   70
Towards his wife. I therefore order thus:
That you bring me the wares here into court
(I have a chest shall hold 'em, as mine own),
And you send me your wife; I'll satisfy her
Myself. I'll do't, and set all straight and right: 75
Justice is blind, but judges have their sight.

DIANA.
And feeling, too, in the Antipodes,
Ha'n't they, my lord?

JOYLESS.   What's that to you, my lady?

WITHIN.
Dismiss the court.

LETOY.
Dismiss the court; cannot you hear the prompter?   80
Ha' you lost your ears, Judge?

BYPLAY.   No, [to *Officer*] dismiss the court.—
Embrace you, friends, and to shun further strife,
See you send me your stuff, and you your wife.

PEREGRINE.
Most admirable justice.

DIANA.   Protest, Extempore played the judge,
And I knew him not all this while.

JOYLESS.   What oversight   85
Was there!

DIANA.   He is a properer man, methinks
Now, than he was before; sure I shall love him.

---

84. *Protest*] i.e., "I protest."

JOYLESS.

Sure, sure, you shall not, shall you?

DIANA.   And I warrant,

By his judgment speech e'en now, he loves a woman well:

For he said, if you noted him, that he   90

Would satisfy the citizen's wife himself.

Methinks a gentlewoman might please him better.

JOYLESS.

How dare you talk so?

Byplay *kneels, and kisses* Peregrine's *hand.*

DIANA.

What's he a-doing now, trow?

PEREGRINE.   Kneel down

Again. Give me a sword, somebody.   95

LETOY.

The king's about to knight him.

BYPLAY.   Let me pray

Your majesty be pleased yet to withhold

That undeserved honor, till you first

Vouchsafe to grace the city with your presence,

Accept one of our hall feasts, and a freedom,   100

And freely use our purse for what great sums

Your majesty will please.

DIANA.   What subjects there are

In the Antipodes.

LETOY.   None in the world so loving.

PEREGRINE.

Give me a sword, I say. Must I call thrice?

LETOY.

No, no, take mine, my liege.

PEREGRINE.   Yours? What are you?   105

DOCTOR.

A loyal lord, one of your subjects, too.

PEREGRINE.

He may be loyal; he's a wondrous plain one.

---

100. *hall feasts*] i.e., in the equivalent of London's Guild Hall.
100. *freedom*] i.e., of the city.

JOYLESS [*aside to* Diana].
    Prithee, Diana, yet let's slip away
    Now while he's busy.
DIANA.   But where's your daughter-in-law?
JOYLESS.
    Gone home, I warrant you, with Mistress Blaze.   110
    Let them be our example.
DIANA.   You are cozen'd.
JOYLESS.
    Y'are an impudent whore.
DIANA.   I know not what I may be
    Made by your jealousy.
PEREGRINE.   I'll none o' this;
    Give me that princely weapon. [*Indicates sword of* Swordbearer.]
LETOY.   Give it him.
SWORDBEARER [*aside to* Letoy].
    It is a property, you know, my lord,   115
    No blade, but a rich scabbard with a lath in't.
LETOY.
    So is the sword of justice, for ought he knows.
PEREGRINE.
    It is enchanted.
BYPLAY.   Yet on me let it fall,
    Since 'tis your highness' will, scabbard and all.
PEREGRINE.
    Rise up, our trusty well-beloved knight.   120
BYPLAY.
    Let me find favor in your gracious sight
    To taste a banquet now, which is prepar'd,
    And shall be by your followers quickly shar'd.
PEREGRINE.
    My followers, where are they?
LETOY [*aside*].   Come, sirs, quickly.

Enter 5 *or* 6 *Courtiers.*

PEREGRINE.
    'Tis well; lead on the way.
DIANA.   And must not we   125

---

118. *enchanted*] i.e., the sword cannot be removed from its scabbard.

Go to the banquet, too?

LETOY.   He must not see

You yet. I have provided otherwise
For both you in my chamber, and from thence
We'll at a window see the rest o'th' play;
Or if you needs, sir, will stay here, you may.   130

JOYLESS.

Was ever man betray'd thus into torment?   *Exeunt.*

[IV.i]   *Enter* Doctor *and* Peregrine.

DOCTOR.

Now, sir, be pleas'd to cloud your princely raiment
With this disguise. Great kings have done the like

Puts on a cloak and hat.

To make discovery of passages
Among the people; thus you shall perceive
What to approve, and what correct among 'em.   5

PEREGRINE.

And so I'll cherish, or severely punish.

Enter an Old Woman *reading; to her, a young* Maid [*with a book*].

DOCTOR.

Stand close, sir, and observe.

OLD WOMAN.

"Royal pastime in a great match between the tanners and
the butchers, six dogs of a side, to play single at the game
bear for fifty pound, and a ten-pound supper for their dogs   10
and themselves. Also you shall see two ten-dog courses at
the great bear."

MAID.

Fie, Granny, fie! Can no persuasions,
Threat'nings, nor blows prevail, but you'll persist

2.1.] Q *prints in margin at right of
ll. 3–4.*

---

129. *window*] presumably one of the windows over right and left stage
doors. A person in one of these balconies could see the inner stage and would
be clearly visible to the spectators in the theater.
[IV.i]
6.1. *reading*] i.e., a handbill.
11. *two ten-dog courses*] two rounds or turns, each consisting of ten dogs
which attack either a bear, lion, or bull.

In these profane and diabolical courses,   15
To follow bearbaitings, when you can scarce
Spell out their bills with spectacles?
OLD WOMAN.   What though
My sight be gone beyond the reach of spectacles
In any print but this, and though I cannot
(No, no, I cannot read your meditations),   20

Strikes down her book.

Yet I can see the royal game played over and over,
And tell which dog does best, without my spectacles.
And though I could not, yet I love the noise;
The noise revives me, and the Bear Garden scent
Refresheth much my smelling.
MAID.   Let me entreat you   25
Forbear such beastly pastimes; th'are satanical.
OLD WOMAN.
Take heed, child, what you say; 'tis the king's game.
PEREGRINE.
What is my game?
DOCTOR.   Bearbaiting, sir, she means.
OLD WOMAN.
"A bear's a princely beast, and one side venison,"
Writ a good author once; you yet want years,   30
And are with baubles pleas'd. I'll see the bears.   *Exit.*
MAID.
And I must bear with it. She's full of wine,
And for the present wilful; but in due

---

15. *profane . . . courses*] a parody of prevalent puritan invective against bearbaiting and other "pernicious and heathenish practices" (e.g., W. Prynne's *Histrio-mastix*, edn. 1633, p. 583).

17. *spectacles*] Spectacle makers in English are first noted around the middle of the seventeenth century.

20.1. *book*] i.e., of meditations.

24. *scent*] Geffrey Minshul in his *Essays and Characters of a Prison and Prisoners* (edn. 1618, sig. B2), compares the stench of a prison with that of the bear gardens: "It is a place that hath more diseases predominant in it, then the Pest-house in the Plague-time, and it stinkes more then the Lord Mayors Dogge-house or Paris-garden in August."

30. *author*] presumably Jonson. See Jonson's *Magnetic Lady* (Induction, ll. 27–30): "Wee are sent unto you, indeed, from the people./ The people! which side of the people?/ The Venison side, if you know it, Boy./ That's the left side."

Season I'll humble her: but we are all
Too subject to infirmity.   35

[IV.ii]   *Enter a young* Gentleman, *and an old* Servingman.

GENTLEMAN.
    Boy. Boy.
SERVINGMAN. Sir.
GENTLEMAN.   Here, take my cloak.
PEREGRINE.
    Boy, did he say?
DOCTOR.   Yes, sir. Old servants are
    But boys to masters, be they ne'er so young.
GENTLEMAN.
    'Tis heavy, and I sweat.
SERVINGMAN.   Take mine and keep you warm then;
    I'll wear yours.
GENTLEMAN.   Out, you varlet;   5
    Dost thou obscure it as thou meantst to pawn it?
    Is this a cloak unworthy of the light?
    Publish it, sirrah. Oh, presumptuous slave,
    Display it on one arm. Oh, ignorance!
SERVINGMAN.
    Pray load your ass yourself, as you would have it.   10
GENTLEMAN.
    Nay, prithee be not angry: thus, and now
    Be sure you bear't at no such distance, but
    As't may be known appendix to this book.
PEREGRINE.
    This custom I have seen with us.
DOCTOR.   Yes, but
    It was deriv'd from the Antipodes.   15
MAID.
    It is a dainty creature, and my blood

---

8. *Publish it*] i.e., display it. Short cloaks, carelessly draped about the
figure in a variety of ways, were fashionable during the reign of Charles I.
Brome probably alludes to one of the fashions in which the cloak is worn
over one shoulder and turned up to show the expensive lining, which was
usually silk, velvet, or a material corresponding to that of the doublet.
    13. *book*] i.e., myself.   16. *dainty*] handsome.

Rebels against the spirit: I must speak to him.

SERVINGMAN.

Sir, here's a gentlewoman makes towards you.

GENTLEMAN.

Me? She's deceived; I am not for her mowing.

MAID.

Fair sir, may you vouchsafe my company?   20

GENTLEMAN.

No truly, I am none of those you look for.
The way is broad enough; unhand me, pray you.

MAID.

Pray sir, be kinder to a lass that loves you.

GENTLEMAN.

Some such there are, but I am none of those.

MAID.

Come, this is but a copy of your countenance.   25
I ha' known you better than you think I do.

GENTLEMAN.

What ha' you known me for?

MAID.   I knew you once
For half a piece, I take it.

GENTLEMAN.   You are deceiv'd
The whole breadth of your nose. I scorn it.

MAID.

Come, be not coy, but send away your servant,   30
And let me gi' you a pint of wine.

GENTLEMAN.   Pray keep
Your courtesy; I can bestow the wine
Upon myself, if I were so dispos'd
To drink in taverns. Fah!

MAID.   Let me bestow't
Upon you at your lodging then; and there   35
Be civilly merry.

GENTLEMAN.   Which if you do,

---

19. *mowing*] copulating (Wright). Cf. Jonson's *A Tale of a Tub*, IV.v.5:
"I am not for your mowing."

25. *copy*] pretence.

28. *piece*] Cf. III.ii.48, n.

29. *whole ... nose*] completely (Baker); more likely antipodal bawdy
(Partridge, p. 159).

My wife shall thank you for it; but your better
Course is to seek one fitter for your turn;
You'll lose your aim in me, and I befriend you
To tell you so.

MAID.   Gip gaffer shotten, fagh!   40
Take that for your coy counsel.   *Kicks.*

GENTLEMAN.   Help! Oh, help!

SERVINGMAN.
What mean you, gentlewoman?

MAID.   That to you, sir.   *Kicks.*

GENTLEMAN.
Oh murder, murder.

SERVINGMAN.   Peace, good Master,
And come away. Some cowardly jade, I warrant,
That durst not strike a woman.   45

[IV.iii]   *Enter* Constable *and* Watch.

CONSTABLE.
What's the matter?

SERVINGMAN.   But and we were your match—

WATCH.
What would you do?
Come, come afore the constable. Now, if
You were her match, what would you do, sir?

MAID.   Do?
They have done too much already, sir; a virgin   *Weeps.*   5
Shall not pass shortly for these streetwalkers,
If some judicious order be not taken.

GENTLEMAN.
Hear me the truth.

CONSTABLE.   Sir, speak to your companions:
I have a wife and daughters, and am bound
By hourly precepts to hear women first,   10
Be't truth, or no truth; therefore, virgin, speak,
And fear no bugbears. I will do thee justice.

---

38. *turn*] "sexual stratagem or bout in love making"; cf. *Cymbeline*
II.iv.142: "Never count the turns" (Partridge, p. 211).
40. *Gip . . . fagh!*] "Get out, you emaciated old grandfather!" *Gaffer* is
Warwickshire dialect for "grandfather" (*OED* and Morgan).

MAID.

   Sir, they assail'd me, and with violent hands,
   When words could not prevail, they would have drawn me
   Aside unto their lust, till I cried murder.   15

GENTLEMAN.

   Protest, sir, as I am a gentleman,
   And as my man's a man, she beat us both,
   Till I cried murder.

SERVINGMAN.   That's the woeful truth on't.

CONSTABLE.

   You are a party, and no witness, sir;
   Besides y'are two, and one is easier   20
   To be believ'd. Moreover as you have the odds
   In number, what were justice if it should not support
   The weaker side? Away with them to the Counter.

PEREGRINE.

   Call you this justice?

DOCTOR.   In th' Antipodes.

PEREGRINE.

   Here's much to be reform'd. Young man, thy virtue   25
   Hath won my favor; go, thou art at large.

               [*The* Gentleman *hesitates.*]

DOCTOR [*aside*].

   Be gone.

GENTLEMAN [*aside*].   He puts me out; my part is now
   To bribe the constable.

DOCTOR [*aside*].   No matter; go.

                     Exeunt Gentleman *and* Servant.

PEREGRINE.

   And you, sir, take that sober-seeming wanton,
   And clap her up, till I hear better of her;   30
   I'll strip you of your office and your ears else.

28.1. *Exeunt*] Baker; *Exit.* Q.

---

  16. *Protest*] cf. III.ix.84, n.
  23. *Counter*] prison, especially for debtors. There were two principal
Counters or Compters in London: in Wood Street, Cheapside, and in the
Poultry.
  31. *ears*] Cf. IV.ix.51, n.

DOCTOR.

    At first show mercy.

PEREGRINE.   They are an ignorant nation,

    And have my pity mingled with correction;

    And, therefore, damsel (for you are the first

    Offender I have noted here, and this   35

    Your first offence, for ought I know)—

MAID.

    Yes, truly.

DOCTOR [*aside to* Maid].   That was well said.

PEREGRINE.

    Go and transgress no more;

    And as you find my mercy sweet, see that

    You be not cruel to your grandmother   40

    When she returns from bearbaiting.

DOCTOR [*aside*].   So, all be gone.

                Exeunt [*all except* Peregrine *and* Doctor].

[IV.iv]

Enter Buff Woman, *her head and face bleeding, and many* Women, *as
from a prize.*

PEREGRINE.

    And what are these?

DOCTOR.

    A woman fencer, that has played a prize,

    It seems, with loss of blood.

PEREGRINE.   It doth amaze me.   *They pass over.*

    What can her husband be, when she's a fencer?

DOCTOR.

    He keeps a school, and teacheth needlework,   5

    Or some such arts which we call womanish.

PEREGRINE.

    'Tis most miraculous and wonderful.

MAN-SCOLD (*within*).

    Rogues, varlets, harlots, ha' you done

    Your worst, or would you drown me? Would you take my life?

WOMEN (*within*).

    Duck him again; duck him again.

IV.iv] *Scene division om. in Q.*

    0.2. *prize*] a fencing contest.

PEREGRINE.   What noise is this?   10
DOCTOR.
    Some man, it seems, that's duck'd for scolding.
PEREGRINE.
    A man for scolding?
DOCTOR.   You shall see.

[IV.v]   *Enter* Women *and* Man-scold.

WOMEN.
    So, so;
    Enough, enough; he will be quiet now.
MAN-SCOLD.
    How know you that, you devil-ridden witch you?
    How, quiet; why quiet? Has not the law passed on me,
    Over and over me, and must I be quiet?   5
1 WOMAN.
    Will you incur the law the second time?
MAN-SCOLD.
    The law's the river, is't? Yes, 'tis a river,
    Through which great men, and cunning, wade, or swim;
    But mean and ignorant must drown in't. No,
    You hags and hellhounds, witches, bitches, all,   10
    That were the law, the judge, and executioners,
    To my vexation, I hope to see
    More flames about your ears than all the water
    You cast me in can quench.
3 WOMAN.
    In with him again; he calls us names.   15
2 WOMAN.
    No, no; I charge ye, no.
MAN-SCOLD.
    Was ever harmless creature so abus'd?
    To be drench'd under water, to learn dumbness
    Amongst the fishes, as I were forbidden
    To use the natural members I was born with,   20
    And of them all the chief that man takes pleasure in,
    The tongue! Oh me, accursed wretch!   *Weeps.*

IV.v] *Misnumbered* Scene 4. *in* Q.

PEREGRINE.   Is this a man?
    I ask not by his beard, but by his tears.

1 WOMAN.
    This shower will spend the fury of his tongue,
    And so the tempest's over.

2 WOMAN.   I am sorry for't;   25
    I would have had him duck'd once more.
    But somebody will shortly raise the storm
    In him again, I hope, for us to make
    More holiday-sport of him.   *Exeunt* [Women *and* Man-scold].

PEREGRINE.   Sure these are dreams,
    Nothing but dreams.

DOCTOR.   No, doubtless we are awake, sir.   30

PEREGRINE.
    Can men and women be so contrary
    In all that we hold proper to each sex?

DOCTOR [*aside*].
    I'm glad he takes a taste of sense in that yet.

PEREGRINE.
    'Twill ask long time and study to reduce
    Their manners to our government.

DOCTOR.   These are   35
    Low things and easy to be qualified.
    But see, sir, here come courtiers; note their manners.

[IV.vi]
Enter a Courtier [*counting his money, and a* Second Courtier *at a distance*].

1 COURTIER.
    This was three shillings yesterday. How now!
    All gone but this? Sixpence for leather soles

---

29. S.D. *Exeunt*] Baker; Exit. Q.   IV.vi] *Misnumbered* Scene 5. *in* Q.

36. *qualified*] regulated.
[IV.vi]
2–3. *leather . . . stockings*] leather soles for slippers or pumps which had soft uppers, often of velvet, worn with expensive silk stockings, fashionable among gallants "for they showed off the comeliness of the wearers's leg much better than did the woolen ones" (Linthicum, p. 261).

To my new, green silk stockings, and a groat
My ordinary in pompions bak'd with onions.
PEREGRINE.

Do such eat pompions?
DOCTOR.   Yes, and clowns muskmellons.   5
1 COURTIER.

Threepence I lost at ninepins; but I got
Six tokens towards that at pigeon-holes.
'Snails, where's the rest? Is my poke bottom broke?
2 COURTIER [coming up behind the first].

What, Jack! A pox o'ertake thee not; how dost?
                              [He] kick[s the First Courtier.]
1 COURTIER.

What with a vengeance ailst? Dost think my breech   10
Is made of bell metal? Take that!   Box o'th' ear.
2 COURTIER.   In earnest?
1 COURTIER.

Yes, till more comes.
2 COURTIER.

Pox rot your hold; let go my lock. D'ee think
Y'are currying of your father's horse again?
1 COURTIER.

I'll teach you to abuse a man behind,   They buffet.   15
Was troubled too much afore.

---

3. *groat*] an English coin (worth fourpence) which ceased to be issued for circulation in 1662 (*OED*).

4. *ordinary*] here the regular daily meal or allowance for food; in the seventeenth century the *ordinary* was usually referred to as an eatinghouse where public meals were provided at fixed prices.

4. *pompions*] pumpkins.

7. *tokens*] "a small piece of brass or copper, generally worth about a farthing, formerly issued by tradesmen" (Halliwell).

7. *pigeon-holes*] a popular outdoor game; "a game like our modern *bagatelle*, where there was a machine with arches for the balls to run through, resembling the cavities made for pigeons in a dove-house" (Halliwell).

8. *poke*] here a pocket, but the word also meant a bag in which a beggar carried his provisions.

11. *In earnest*] (1) seriously; (2) as a guarantee that the rest will be paid in full.

13. *lock*] Long flowing locks reaching the shoulders were the fashion for men from 1628–1660.

[IV.vii]   *Enter* Third Courtier.

3 COURTIER.

    Hey, there boys, there.

    Good boys are good boys still. There, Will; there, Jack.

    [*The* Second Courtier *knocks down the* First.]

    Not a blow! Now he's down.

2 COURTIER.   'Twere base; I scorn't.

1 COURTIER.

    There's as proud fall, as stand in court or city.

3 COURTIER.

    That's well said, Will. Troth, I commend you both.   5

    How fell you out? I hope in no great anger.

2 COURTIER.

    For mine own part, I vow I was in jest.

1 COURTIER.

    But I have told you twice and once, Will, jest not

    With me behind. I never could endure

    (Not of a boy) to put up things behind: 10

    And that my tutor knew; I had bin a scholar else.

    Besides, you know my sword was nock'd i'th' fashion,

    Just here behind, for my back-guard and all;

    And yet you would do't.

    I had as lief you would take a knife—

3 COURTIER.   Come, come,   15

    Y'are friends. Shake hands; I'll give you half a dozen

    At the next ale house, to set all right and straight,

    And a new song, a dainty one; here 'tis.   [*Shows*] *a ballad.*

1 COURTIER.

    Oh, thou art happy that canst read;

    I would buy ballads, too, had I thy learning.   20

IV.vii] *Misnumbered* Sc. 6. *in* Q.

---

    8. *once*] i.e., once for all.

    12. *nock'd*] notched; also an erotic homosexual reference to "a man's posterior, from being cleft" (Nares), a play on "behind" (l. 10). Cf. Brome's *Court Beggar* (edn. 1653, sig. Q3ᵛ: "Why dost thou weare a Sword? Only to hurt mens feet that kick thee?"

    16. *dozen*] i.e., mugs of ale.

    18. *dainty*] excellent.

    20. *ballads*] normally for common people, not courtiers.

3 COURTIER.

Come, we burn daylight, and the ale may sour.

Exeunt [Courtiers].

PEREGRINE.

Call you these courtiers? They are rude silken clowns,
As coarse within as watermen or carmen.

DOCTOR.

Then look on these; here are of those conditions.

[IV.viii]   *Enter* Carman *and* Waterman.

WATERMAN.

Sir, I am your servant.

CARMAN.   I am much oblig'd,
Sir, by the plenteous favors your humanity
And noble virtue have conferr'd upon me,
To answer with my service your deservings.

WATERMAN.

You speak what I should say. Be therefore pleas'd   5
T'unload, and lay the weight of your commands
Upon my care to serve you.

CARMAN.   Still your courtesies,
Like waves of a spring tide, o'erflow the banks
Of your abundant store; and from your channel,
Or stream of fair affections, you cast forth   10
Those sweet refreshings on me (that were else
But sterile earth) which cause a gratitude
To grow upon me, humble, yet ambitious
In my devoir to do you best of service.

WATERMAN.

I shall no more extend my utmost labor,   15
With oar and sail to gain the livelihood
Of wife and children than to set ashore
You and your faithful honorers at the haven
Of your best wishes.

IV.viii] *Q prints scene division
(misnumbered* Scen. 7.) *in margin of
IV.vii.23.*

---

21. *burn daylight*] waste time.

CARMAN.   Sir, I am no less
   Ambitious to be made the happy means,   20
   With whip and whistle, to draw up or drive
   All your detractors to the gallows.

[IV.ix]   *Enter* Sedanman.

WATERMAN.
   See,
   Our noble friend.
SEDANMAN.   Right happily encounter'd;
   I am the just admirer of your virtues.
CARMAN. WATERMAN.
   We are, in all, your servants.
SEDANMAN.   I was in quest
   Of such elect society, to spend   5
   A dinner time withal.
CARMAN. WATERMAN.   Sir, we are for you.
SEDANMAN.
   Three are the golden number in a tavern;
   And at the next of best, with the best meat
   And wine the house affords (if you so please)
   We will be competently merry. I   10
   Have receiv'd, lately, letters from beyond seas,
   Importing much of the occurrences
   And passages of foreign states. The knowledge
   Of all I shall impart to you.
WATERMAN.   And I
   Have all the new advertisements from both   15
   Our universities of what has passed
   The most remarkably of late.

IV.ix] *Misnumbered* Scene 8. *in* Q.   0.1.] *Q prints in margin at right of l. 1.*
                                             4, 6, S.P.] *Baker; 2. Q.*

───

   2. *friend*] The current contention between watermen and the sedanmen
is evident from a reference in Brome's *Court Beggar* (I.i, sig. O1ᵛ), where the
projector suggests a "new project for buylding a new Theatre or Play-house
Upon the Thames on Barges or flat boats to helpe the watermen out of the
losse they've suffer'd by Sedans." See also J. Taylor's "The World runnes
on wheeles" (in Taylor, p. 232).
   8. *next of best*] i.e., the nearest and best tavern.
   15–16. *new ... universities*] latest notices or information from Oxford
and Cambridge.

CARMAN.   And from
     The court I have the news at full,
     Of all that was observable this progress.
PEREGRINE.   From court?
DOCTOR.
     Yes, sir; they know not there they have   20
     A new king here at home.
SEDANMAN.   'Tis excellent!
     We want but now the news-collecting gallant
     To fetch his dinner, and materials
     For his this week's dispatches.
WATERMAN.   I dare think,
     The meat and news being hot upon the table,   25
     He'll smell his way to't.
SEDANMAN.
     Please you to know yours, sir?
CARMAN.   Sir, after you.
SEDANMAN.
     Excuse me.
WATERMAN.   By no means, sir.
CARMAN.
     Sweet sir, lead on.
SEDANMAN.   It shall be as your servant
     Then, to prepare your dinner.

                    [*He leads the way.*]

WATERMAN.   Pardon me.   30
CARMAN.
     Insooth, I'll follow you.
WATERMAN.   Yet 'tis my obedience.
                    Exeunt, [*the* Waterman *before the* Carman].
PEREGRINE.
     Are these but laboring men, and tother courtiers?
DOCTOR.
     'Tis common here, sir, for your watermen
     To write most learnedly, when your courtier
     Has scarce ability to read.
PEREGRINE.   Before I reign   35
     A month among them, they shall change their notes,

---

19. *progress*] royal journey.

Or I'll ordain a course to change their coats.
I shall have much to do in reformation.

DOCTOR.

Patience and counsel will go through it, sir.

PEREGRINE.

What if I crav'd a counsel from New England?   40
The old will spare me none.

DOCTOR [*aside*].   Is this man mad?
My cure goes fairly on. —Do you marvel that
Poor men outshine the courtiers? Look you, sir,
A sick man giving counsel to a physician:

These persons pass over the stage in couples, according as he describes them.

And there's a puritan tradesman teaching a   45
Great traveler to lie; that ballad woman
Gives light to the most learned antiquary
In all the kingdom.

BALLAD WOMAN.   Buy new ballads, come.

DOCTOR.

A natural fool, there, giving grave instructions
T'a lord ambassador; that's a schismatic,   50
Teaching a scrivener to keep his ears;
A parish clerk, there, gives the rudiments
Of military discipline to a general;
And there's a basket maker confuting Bellarmine.

44.1.] *Q prints in margin at right
of ll.* 47–52.

---

39. *go through*] execute.

41. *spare me none*] Charles I dissolved Parliament in 1629 and did not call another until 1640. Men were forbidden to speak of its reassembling.

49. *natural fool*] a born idiot, not the professional clown (*OED*).

51. *scrivener . . . ears*] William Prynne, a Presbyterian lawyer and pamphleteer, for an indirect attack upon the Queen in his *Histriomastix* (1634), was sentenced by the Star Chamber to suffer many indignities, among which were the loss of both ears, and later, in 1637, the loss of the stumps of both ears for his continued writing from prison. Dishonest scriveners suffered the same penalty.

54. *Bellarmine*] Cardinal Bellarmine (1542–1621), the great opponent of the Protestant Party. He was famous for his theological disputes with James I over the power of the Pope in political spheres. Among his more important controversial works were his *Disputations de Contraverssi fidei* (1581).

PEREGRINE.
   Will you make me mad?
DOCTOR.   We are sail'd, I hope,   55
   Beyond the line of madness. Now, sir, see
   A statesman, studious for the commonwealth,
   Solicited by projectors of the country.

[IV.x]
Enter Byplay *like a statesman;* 3 *or* 4 Projectors *with bundles of papers.*

BYPLAY.
   Your projects are all good; I like them well,
   Especially these two: this for th'increase of wool,
   And this for the destroying of mice. They're good,
   And grounded on great reason.—As for yours,
   For putting down the infinite use of jacks   5
   (Whereby the education of young children
   In turning spits is greatly hinder'd),
   It may be look'd into. —And yours against
   The multiplicity of pocket watches
   (Whereby much neighborly familiarity,   10
   By asking, "What d' ye guess it is o'clock?"
   Is lost when every puny clerk can carry
   The time o'th' day in's breeches): this and these
   Hereafter may be look'd into. For present,
   This for the increase of wool—that is to say,   15
   By flaying of live horses and new covering them
   With sheepskins, I do like exceedingly.
   And this for keeping of tame owls in cities
   To kill up rats and mice, whereby all cats

IV.x] *Q prints scene division (mis-*   0.1.] *Q prints in margin at right of*
numbered Sc. 9.) *in margin at right of*   *IV.ix.55–58 and IV.x.1.*
IV.ix.54.

58. *projectors*] promoters of moneymaking projects. A serious abuse of the time, scenes depicting projectors presenting their projects were often included in current drama, e.g., Shakerly Marmion's *Holland's Leaguer* (I.v.), edn. 1632, and Brome's *Court Beggar* (I.i), edn. 1653.
[IV.x]
5. *jacks*] "When instruments for pulling off boots and turning spits were introduced, they were given the name Jack—formerly applied to the foot-boys who performed these tasks" (Nares, quoted by Baker).

May be destroyed, as an especial means   20
To prevent witchcraft and contagion.

PEREGRINE.

Here's a wise business!

PROJECTOR.   Will your honor now
Be pleas'd to take into consideration
The poor men's suits for briefs to get relief
By common charity throughout the kingdom,   25
Towards recovery of their lost estates?

BYPLAY.

What are they? Let me hear.

PROJECTOR.

First, here's a gamester, that sold house and land
To the known value of five thousand pounds,
And by misfortune of the dice lost all,   30
To his extreme undoing, having neither
A wife or child to succour him.

BYPLAY.   A bachelor?

PROJECTOR.

Yes, my good lord.

BYPLAY.   And young, and healthful?

PROJECTOR.

Yes.

BYPLAY.   Alas, 'tis lamentable; he deserves much pity.

PEREGRINE.

How's this?

DOCTOR.   Observe him further, pray sir.   35

PROJECTOR.

Then, here's a bawd, of sixty odd years standing.

BYPLAY.

How old was she when she set up?

PROJECTOR.   But four
And twenty, my good lord. She was both ware
And merchant, flesh and butcher (as they say)
For the first twelve years of her housekeeping: 40
She's now upon fourscore, and has made markets
Of twice four thousand choice virginities,
And twice their number of indifferent gear.

_____

43. *gear*] kind or sort (Baker).

(No riffraff was she ever known to cope for.)
Her life is certified here by the justices   45
Adjacent to her dwelling—

BYPLAY.   She is decay'd?

PROJECTOR.
  Quite trade fallen, my good lord, now in her dotage,
  And desperately undone by riot.

BYPLAY.   'Las good woman.

PROJECTOR.
  She has consum'd in prodigal feasts and fiddlers,
  And lavish lendings to debauch'd comrades,   50
  That suck'd her purse, in jewels, plate, and money
  To the full value of six thousand pounds.

BYPLAY.
  She shall have a collection, and deserves it.

PEREGRINE.
  'Tis monstrous, this.

PROJECTOR.   Then here are divers more,
  Of panders, cheaters, house and highway robbers,   55
  That have got great estates in youth and strength,
  And wasted all as fast in wine and harlots
  Till age o'ertook 'em, and disabled them
  For getting more.

BYPLAY.   For such the law provides
  Relief within those counties where they practic'd.   60

PEREGRINE.
  Ha! What, for thieves?

DOCTOR.   Yes, their law punisheth
  The robb'd, and not the thief, for surer warning
  And the more safe prevention. I have seen
  Folks whipp'd for losing of their goods and money,
  And the pickpockets cherish'd.

BYPLAY.   The weal public,   65
  As it severely punisheth their neglect,
  Undone by fire ruins, shipwreck, and the like,
  With whips, with brands, and loss of careless ears,
  Imprisonment, banishment, and sometimes death;

---

68. *careless ears*] i.e., ears belonging to the careless.

And carefully maintaineth houses of correction   70
For decay'd scholars and maim'd soldiers;
So doth it find relief and almshouses
For such as liv'd by rapine and by cozenage.
PEREGRINE.
Still worse and worse! Abominable, horrid!
PROJECTOR.
Yet here is one, my lord, 'bove all the rest,   75
Whose services have generally bin known,
Though now he be a spectacle of pity.
BYPLAY.   Who's that?
PROJECTOR.
The captain of the cutpurses, my lord,
That was the best at's art that ever was,
Is fallen to great decay by the dead palsy   80
In both his hands, and craves a large collection.
BYPLAY.
I'll get it him.
PEREGRINE.   You shall not get it him.
Do you provide whips, brands, and ordain death
For men that suffer under fire or shipwreck
The loss of all their honest gotten wealth,   85
And find relief for cheaters, bawds, and thieves?
I'll hang ye all.
BYPLAY.   Mercy, great King.
OMNES.   Oh mercy.
BYPLAY.
Let not our ignorance suffer in your wrath
Before we understand your highness' laws;
We went by custom, and the warrant which   90
We had in your late predecessor's reign;
But let us know your pleasure, you shall find
The state and commonwealth in all obedient
To alter custom, law, religion, all,
To be conformable to your commands.   95
PEREGRINE.
'Tis a fair protestation, and my mercy
Meets your submission. See you merit it
In your conformity.

BYPLAY.   Great sir, we shall.

> Letoy, Diana, Joyless *appear above.*

In sign whereof we lacerate these papers,
And lay our necks beneath your kingly feet.   100

PEREGRINE.

Stand up; you have our favor.

DIANA.   And mine, too!

Never was such an actor as Extempore!

JOYLESS.

You were best to fly out of the window to him.

DIANA.

Methinks I am even light enough to do it.

JOYLESS.

I could find in my heart to quoit thee at him.   105

DIANA.

So he would catch me in his arms, I car'd not.

LETOY.

Peace, both of you, or you'll spoil all.

BYPLAY.   Your grace

Abounds—abounds—Your grace—I say, abounds—

LETOY.

Pox o' your mumbling chops; is your brain dry?
Do your pump?

DIANA.   He has done much, my lord, and may   110
Hold out a little.

LETOY.   Would you could hold your peace
So long.

DIANA.   Do you sneap me, too, my lord.

JOYLESS.

Ha, ha, ha!

LETOY.   Blockhead!

98.1. *above*] at a chamber window (cf. III.ix.129, n.).
99. *lacerate*] destroy, i.e., tear briefs containing poor men's suits and papers containing projects.
104. *light*] (1) not heavy; (2) wanton.
105. *quoit*] throw (Onions).
112. *sneap*] chide, rebuke.

JOYLESS.   I hope his hotter zeal to's actors
Will drive out my wife's love heat.
DIANA.   I had
No need to come hither to be sneap'd.   115
LETOY.
Hoyday! The rest will all be lost. [*To* Joyless.]   We now
Give over the play, and do all by extempore
For your son's good, to sooth him into's wits.
If you'll mar all, you may. [*Aside to* Byplay.]   Come
    nearer, cockscomb;
Ha' you forgotten, puppy, my instructions   120
Touching his subjects and his marriage?
BYPLAY [*aside*].
I have all now, my lord.
PEREGRINE.   What voice was that?
BYPLAY.
A voice out of the clouds, that doth applaud
Your highness' welcome to your subjects' loves.
LETOY.
So, now he's in. [*To* Joyless *and* Diana.]   Sit still, I must
    go down   125
And set out things in order.   *Exit.*
BYPLAY.
A voice that doth inform me of the tidings
Spread through your kingdom of your great arrival,
And of the general joy your people bring
To celebrate the welcome of their king.   *Shouts within.* 130
Heark how the country shouts with joyful votes,
Rending the air with music of their throats.   *Drum & Trumpets.*
Heark how the soldier with his martial noise
Threatens your foes, to fill your crown with joys.
Heark how the city with loud harmony   *Hautboys.* 135
Chants a free welcome to your majesty.
Heark how the court prepares your grace to meet   *Soft music.*
With solemn music, state, and beauty sweet.

116–117. Hoyday ... over] *this
edn.; one line in Q.*

116. *Hoyday*] obsolete form of heyday.   125. *in*] i.e., in character.
133. *noise*] music.   135.S.D. *Hautboys*] cf. I.v.64.1, n.

[IV.xi]

The soft music playing, enter by two and two divers courtiers; Martha *after
them, like a queen, between two boys in robes, her train borne up by* Barbara.
All the lords kneel and kiss Peregrine's *hand.* Martha *approaching, he
starts back, but is drawn on by* Byplay *and the* Doctor. Letoy *enters and
mingles with the rest, and seems to instruct them all.*

DIANA.

    Oh, here's a stately show! Look, Master Joyless:
    Your daughter-in-law presented like a queen
    Unto your son; I warrant now he'll love her.

JOYLESS.

    A queen?

DIANA.   Yes, yes, and Mistress Blaze is made
    The mother of her maids, if she have any;   5
    Perhaps the Antipodean court has none.
    See, see, with what a majesty he receives 'em.

SONG

    Health, wealth, and joy our wishes bring,
    All in a welcome to our king:
      May no delight be found,   10
      Wherewith he be not crown'd.
    Apollo with the Muses,
    Who arts divine infuses,
    With their choice garlands deck his head;
    Love and the graces make his bed;   15
    And to crown all, let Hymen to his side
    Plant a delicious, chaste, and fruitful bride.

BYPLAY.

    Now, sir, be happy in a marriage choice
    That shall secure your title of a king.
    See, sir, your state presents to you the daughter,   20
    The only child and heir apparent of
    Our late deposed and deceased sovereign,
    Who with his dying breath bequeath'd her to you.

IV.xi] *Misnumbered* Sce. 10. *in* Q.

---

   5. *mother ... maids*] i.e., head of the maids of honor in a royal house
(*OED*).
   16. *Hymen*] god of marriage.

PEREGRINE.

A crown secures not an unlawful marriage.

I have a wife already.

DOCTOR.   No, you had, sir;   25

But she's deceas'd.

PEREGRINE.   How know you that?

DOCTOR.

By sure advertisement; and that her fleeting spirit

Is flown into and animates this princess.

PEREGRINE.

Indeed, she's wondrous like her.

DOCTOR.   Be not slack

T'embrace and kiss her, sir.   *He kisses her and retires.*

MARTHA.   He kisses sweetly;   30

And that is more than e'er my husband did.

But more belongs than kissing to child-getting;

And he's so like my husband, if you note him,

That I shall but lose time and wishes by him.

No, no, I'll none of him.   35

BARBARA.

I'll warrant you he shall fulfil your wishes.

MARTHA.

Oh, but try him you first, and then tell me.

BARBARA.

There's a new way, indeed, to choose a husband!

Yet 'twere a good one to bar fool-getting.

DOCTOR.

Why do you stand aloof, sir?

PEREGRINE.   Mandeville writes   40

Of people near the Antipodes call'd Gadlibriens:

Where on the wedding night the husband hires

Another man to couple with his bride,

To clear the dangerous passage of a maidenhead.

DOCTOR.

'Slid, he falls back again to Mandeville madness.   45

PEREGRINE.

She may be of that serpentine generation

That stings oft times to death (as Mandeville writes).

---

41. *Gadlibriens*] described in Mandeville, Chap. XCII, sig. S3.

DOCTOR.

She's no Gadlibrien, sir, upon my knowledge.
You may as safely lodge with her as with
A maid of our own nation. Besides,   50
You shall have ample counsel: for the present,
Receive her, and entreat her to your chapel.

BYPLAY.

For safety of your kingdom, you must do it.
                Hautboys. Exeunt in state as Letoy *directs. Manet* Letoy.

LETOY.

So, so, so, so; this yet may prove a cure.

DIANA.

See, my lord now is acting by himself.   55

LETOY.

And Letoy's wit cried up triumphant, ho!
Come, Master Joyless and your wife, come down
Quickly; your parts are next. I had almost
Forgot to send my chaplain after them.
You, Domine, where are you?   60
                          [*Exeunt above* Joyless *and* Diana.]

[IV.xii]   *Enter* Quailpipe *in a fantastical shape.*

QUAILPIPE.

Here, my lord.

LETOY.

What, in that shape?
QUAILPIPE.   'Tis for my part, my lord,
Which is not all perform'd.

LETOY.

It is, sir, and the play for this time. We
Have other work in hand.
QUAILPIPE.   Then have you lost   5
Action (I dare be bold to speak it) that

53.1. *Exeunt*] *Baker; Exit Q.*
53.1.] *Q prints in margin at right of*
ll. 53–57.
IV.xii] *Q prints scene division (mis-*
numbered Sce. 11.) *in margin at right*

of IV.xi.58.
0.1.] *Q prints in margin at right of*
IV.*xi.59–60.*
2. S.P. QUAILPIPE] *Baker; Chap.*
(i.e., Chaplain)Q.

0.1. *shape*] costume.

Most of my coat could hardly imitate.
LETOY.

Go, shift your coat, sir, or for expedition,
Cover it with your own, due to your function.
Follies, as well as vices, may be hid so: 10
Your virtue is the same. Dispatch, and do
As Doctor Hughball shall direct you. Go.   *Exit* Quailpipe.

[IV.xiii]   *Enter* Joyless, Diana.

LETOY.

Now, Master Joyless, do you note the progress
And the fair issue likely to ensue
In your son's cure? Observe the doctor's art.
First, he has shifted your son's known disease
Of madness into folly, and has wrought him   5
As far short of a competent reason as
He was of late beyond it; as a man
Infected by some foul disease is drawn
By physic into an anatomy,
Before flesh fit for health can grow to rear him,   10
So is a madman made a fool, before
Art can take hold of him to wind him up
Into his proper center, or the medium
From which he flew beyond himself. The doctor
Assures me now, by what he has collected   15
As well from learned authors as his practice,
That his much troubled and confused brain
Will by the real knowledge of a woman
Now opportunely ta'en, be by degrees
Settled and rectified, with the helps beside   20
Of rest and diet, which he'll administer.

IV.xiii] *Misnumbered* Sce. 12. *in Q*.   0.1.] *Q prints in margin at right of
ll. 1–2.*

7. *of my coat*] garb, indicating profession, class, order, sort, or party
(*OED*).
9. *function*] role or part.
[IV.xiii]
9. *anatomy*] skeleton.

DIANA.

> But 'tis the real knowledge of the woman
> (Carnal, I think you mean) that carries it.

LETOY.   Right, right.

DIANA.

> Nay, right or wrong, I could even wish
> If he were not my husband's son, the doctor   25
> Had made myself his recipe, to be the means
> Of such a cure.

JOYLESS.   How, how?

DIANA.

> Perhaps that course might cure your madness, too,
> Of jealousy, and set all right on all sides.
> Sure, if I could but make him such a fool,   30
> He would forgo his madness, and be brought
> To Christian sense again.

JOYLESS.   Heaven grant me patience,

> And send us to my country home again.

DIANA.

> Besides, the young man's wife's as mad as he.
> What wise work will they make!

LETOY.   The better; fear't not: 35

> Bab Blaze shall give her counsel; and the youth
> Will give her royal satisfaction,
> Now, in this kingly humor. —[*Aside to* Diana.]   I have a way
> To cure your husband's jealousy myself.

DIANA [*aside to* Letoy].

> Then I am friends again; even now I was not   40
> When you sneap'd me, my lord.

LETOY [*aside to* Diana].   That you must pardon.—

> Come, Mr. Joyless. The new married pair
> Are towards bed by this time; we'll not trouble them,
> But keep a house-side to ourselves. Your lodging
> Is decently appointed.

JOYLESS.   Sure your lordship   45

> Means not to make your house our prison.

LETOY.   By

---

45. *decently*] suitably.

My lordship but I will for this one night.
See, sir, the keys are in my hand. Y'are up,
As I am true Letoy. Consider, sir,
The strict necessity that ties you to't,   50
As you expect a cure upon your son. —
Come, Lady, see your chamber.

DIANA.   I do wait
Upon your lordship.

JOYLESS.   I both wait, and watch;
Never was man so master'd by his match.   *Exeunt omnes.*

[V.i]   [*Enter*] Joyless, *with a light in his hand.*

JOYLESS.
Diana! Ho! Where are you? She is lost.
Here is no further passage. All's made fast.
This was the bawdy way by which she scap'd
My narrow watching. Have you privy posterns
Behind the hangings in your strangers' chambers?   5
She's lost from me, forever. Why then seek I?
Oh my dull eyes, to let her slip so from ye,
To let her have her lustful will upon me!
Is this the hospitality of lords?
Why, rather, if he did intend my shame   10
And her dishonor, did he not betray me
From her out of his house, to travel in
The bare suspicion of their filthiness;
But hold me a nose witness to its rankness?
No! This is sure the lordlier way, and makes   15
The act more glorious in my sufferings. Oh!
May my hot curses on their melting pleasures
Cement them so together in their lust
That they may never part, but grow one monster.

[V.ii]   *Enter* Barbara.

BARBARA [*aside*].
Good gentleman! He is at his prayers now,

---

48. *Y'are up*] i.e., you're caught.
54. *match*] wife.

For his mad son's good night-work with his bride.
Well fare your heart, sir; you have pray'd to purpose,
But not all night, I hope. Yet sure he has;
He looks so wild for lack of sleep. —Y'are happy, sir.   5
Your prayers are heard, no doubt, for I'm persuaded
You have a child got you tonight.

JOYLESS.   Is't gone
So far, do you think?

BARBARA.   I cannot say how far.
Not fathom deep, I think; but to the scantling
Of a child-getting, I dare well imagine.   10
For which, as you have pray'd, forget not, sir,
To thank the lord o'th' house.

JOYLESS.   For getting me
A child? Why I am none of his great lordship's tenants,
Nor of his followers, to keep his bastards.
Pray stay a little.

BARBARA.   I should go tell my lord   15
The news: he longs to know how things do pass.

JOYLESS.
Tell him I take it well, and thank him.
I did before despair of children, I.
But I'll go wi' ye, and thank him.

BARBARA.   Sure his joy
Has madded him; here's more work for the doctor.   20

JOYLESS.
But tell me first: were you their bawd that speak this?

BARBARA.
What mean you with that dagger?

JOYLESS.   Nothing, I
But play with't. Did you see the passages
Of things? I ask, were you their bawd?

BARBARA.   Their bawd?
I trust she is no bawd that sees and helps   25
(If need require) an ignorant lawful pair
To do their best.

---

9. *scantling*] possible pun on a term used in archery, applied "to the distance from the mark, within which a shot was not regarded as a miss"
(*OED*).

JOYLESS.   Lord's actions all are lawful.
  And how? And how?
BARBARA.   These old folks love to hear.
  I'll tell you, sir—and yet I will not neither.
JOYLESS.
  Nay, pray thee out with't.
BARBARA.   Sir, they went to bed.   30
JOYLESS.
  To bed! Well, on.
BARBARA.   On? They were off, sir, yet;
  And yet a good while after. They were both
  So simple that they knew not what nor how,
  For she's, sir, a pure maid.
JOYLESS.   Who dost thou speak of?
BARBARA.
  I'll speak no more, 'less you can look more tamely.   35
JOYLESS.
  Go, bring me to 'em then. Bawd, will you go?

                    [*Threatens her with his dagger.*]

BARBARA.
  Ah——

[V.iii]   *Enter* Byplay *and holds* Joyless.

BYPLAY.
  What ail you, sir? Why bawd? Whose bawd is she?
JOYLESS.
  You lord's bawd, and my wife's.
BYPLAY.   You are jealous mad.
  Suppose your wife be missing at your chamber,
  And my lord, too, at his; they may be honest,
  If not, what's that to her, or you, I pray,   5
  Here in my lord's own house?
JOYLESS.   Brave, brave, and monstrous!
BYPLAY.
  She has not seen them. I heard all your talk.
  The child she intimated is your grandchild
  In posse, sir, and of your son's begetting.

---

9. *In posse*] i.e., in the state of being possible.

BARBARA.

    Ay, I'll be sworn I meant and said so, too!   10

JOYLESS.

    Where is my wife?

BYPLAY.   I can give no account.

    If she be with my lord I dare not trouble 'em,

    Nor must you offer at it: no, nor stab yourself,

           Byplay takes away his dagger.

    But come with me. I'll counsel, or at least

    Govern you better. She may be, perhaps,   15

    About the bride-chamber to hear some sport,

    For you can make her none, 'las, good old man—

JOYLESS.

    I'm most insufferably abus'd.

BYPLAY.   —Unless

    The killing of yourself may do't, and that

    I would forbear, because perhaps 'twould please her.   20

JOYLESS.

    If fire, or water, poison, cord, or steel,

    Or any means be found to do it, I'll do it;

    Not to please her, but rid me of my torment.

BYPLAY.

    I have more care and charge of you than so.

           Exeunt Joyless *and* Byplay.

BARBARA.

    What an old desperate man is this, to make   25

    Away yourself for fear of being a cuckold!

    If every man that is, or that but knows

    Himself to be o'th'order, should do so,

    How many desolate widows would here be;

    They are not all of that mind. Here's my husband.   30

[V.iv]   *Enter* Blaze *with a habit in his hand.*

BLAZE.

    Bab! Art thou here?

BARBARA.   Look well. How thinkst thou, Tony?

---

10. Ay] *this edn.;* I *Q.*   24.1.] *Q prints in margin at right of*
                                         ll. 23–24.

Hast not thou neither slept tonight?

BLAZE.   Yes, yes.

I lay with the butler. Who was thy bedfellow?

BARBARA.

You know I was appointed to sit up.

BLAZE.

Yes, with the doctor in the bride-chamber.   5
But had you two no waggery? Ha!

BARBARA.   Why, how now, Tony?

BLAZE.

Nay, facks, I am not jealous.
Thou knowst I was cur'd long since, and how.
I jealous! I an ass. A man sha'n't ask
His wife shortly how such a gentleman does,   10
Or how such a gentleman did, or which did best,
But she must think him jealous.

BARBARA.   You need not: for
If I were now to die on't, nor the doctor
Nor I came in a bed tonight. I mean
Within a bed.

BLAZE.   Within, or without, or over, or under,   15
I have no time to think o' such poor things.

BARBARA.

What's that thou carriest, Tony?

BLAZE.   Oh ho, Bab.

This is a shape.

BARBARA.   A shape? What shape, I prithee, Tony?

BLAZE.

Thou'lt see me in't anon, but shalt not know me
From the starkst fool i'th' town. And I must dance   20
Naked in't, Bab.

BARBARA.   Will here be dancing, Tony?

BLAZE.

Yes, Bab. My lord gave order for't last night.
It should ha' bin i'th' play; but because that
Was broke off, he will ha't today.

BARBARA.   Oh Tony.
I did not see thee act i'th' play.

_____

7. *facks*] by my faith (Baker).

BLAZE.   Oh, but   25
  I did though, Bab, two mutes.
BARBARA.   What, in those breeches?
BLAZE.
  Fie, fool; thou understandst not what a mute is.
  A mute is a dumb speaker in the play.
BARBARA.
  Dumb speaker! That's a bull. Thou wert the bull
  Then, in the play. Would I had seen thee roar.   30
BLAZE.
  That's a bull, too, as wise as you are, Bab.
  A mute is one that acteth speakingly,
  And yet says nothing. I did two of them.
  The sage man-midwife, and the basket maker.
BARBARA.
  Well, Tony, I will see thee in this thing.   35
  And 'tis a pretty thing.
BLAZE.   Prithee, good Bab,
  Come in, and help me on with't in our tiring house.
  And help the gentlemen, my fellow dancers,
  And thou shalt then see all our things, and all
  Our properties, and practice to the music.   40
BARBARA.
  Oh, Tony, come; I long to be at that.   *Exeunt.*

[V.v]   [*Enter*] Letoy *and* Diana.

DIANA.
  My lord, your strength and violence prevail not.
  There is a providence above my virtue,
  That guards me from the fury of your lust.
LETOY.
  Yet, yet, I prithee yield. Is it my person
  That thou despisest? See, here's wealthy treasure,   5

        [*Reveals*] *a table set forth, covered with treasure.*

  Jewels that Cleopatra would have left

V.v] *Misnumbered* Scene 2. *in* Q.   5.1.] Q *prints in margin at right of*
                                         ll. 5–7.

───

  26. *mutes*] (1) a silent actor; (2) act of voiding.

Her Marcus for.

DIANA.   My lord, 'tis possible
That she who leaves a husband, may be bought
Out of a second friendship.

LETOY.   Had stout Tarquin
Made such an offer, he had done no rape,   10
For Lucrece had consented, sav'd her own,
And all those lives that followed in her cause.

DIANA.

Yet then she had been a loser.

LETOY.   Wouldst have gold?
Mammon nor Pluto's self should overbid me,
For I'ld give all. First, let me rain a shower   15
To outvie that which overwhelmed Danaë;
And after that another; a full river
Shall from my chests perpetually flow
Into thy store.

DIANA.   I have not much lov'd wealth,
But have not loath'd the sight of it till now   20
That you have soil'd it with that foul opinion
Of being the price of virtue. Though the metal
Be pure and innocent in itself, such use
Of it is odious, indeed damnable,
Both to the seller and the purchaser: 25
Pity it should be so abus'd. It bears
A stamp upon't, which but to clip is treason.
'Tis ill us'd there, where law the life controls;
Worse, where 'tis made a salary for souls.

LETOY.

Deny'st thou wealth? Wilt thou have pleasure then   30
Given, and ta'en freely, without all condition?
I'll give thee such, as shall (if not exceed)
Be at the least comparative with those

---

7. *Marcus*] Mark Antony.

15. *shower*] the shower of gold, in which form Zeus, according to Greek mythology, visited Danaë while she was shut up in a brazen tower by her father.

27. *to clip*] (1) to deface current coin (metal) by fraudulently paring edges; (2) to embrace amorously (Partridge, p. 88).

29. *salary*] payment.

Which Jupiter got the demigods with; and
Juno was mad she miss'd.

DIANA.   My lord, you may   35
Gloss o'er and gild the vice, which you call pleasure,
With god-like attributes, when it is at best
A sensuality so far below
Dishonorable that it is mere beastly;
Which reason ought to abhor; and I detest it   40
More than your former hated offers.

LETOY.   Lastly,
Wilt thou have honor! I'll come closer to thee
(For now the flames of love grow higher in me,
And I must perish in them, or enjoy thee);
Suppose I find by power, or law, or both,   45
A means to make thee mine, by freeing
Thee from thy present husband.

DIANA.   Hold, stay there.
Now should you utter volumes of persuasions,
Lay the whole world of riches, pleasures, honors
Before me in full grant, that one last word   50
"Husband," and from your own mouth spoke, confutes
And vilifies even all. The very name
Of husband, rightly weigh'd and well remember'd,
Without more law or discipline, is enough
To govern womankind in due obedience,   55
Master all loose affections, and remove
Those idols which too much, too many love,
And you have set before me to beguile
Me of the faith I owe him. But remember
You grant I have a husband; urge no more;   60
I seek his love. 'Tis fit he loves no whore.

LETOY.
This is not yet the way. You have seen, Lady,
My ardent love, which you do seem to slight,
Though to my death, pretending zeal to your husband.
My person, nor my proffers are so despicable   65
But that they might (had I not vow'd affection

48. you] *Baker;* I *Q.*

39. *mere*] absolutely, completely.

Entirely to yourself) have met with th'embraces
Of greater persons, no less fair, that can,
Too (if they please), put on formality,
And talk in as divine a strain as you.   70
This is not earnest; make my word but good
Now with a smile, I'll give thee a thousand pound.
Look o' my face. Come. Prithee, look and laugh not.
Yes, laugh, and dar'st. Dimple this cheek a little;
I'll nip it else.

DIANA.   I pray forbear, my lord: 75
I'm past a child, and will be made no wanton.

LETOY.
How can this be? So young, so vigorous,
And so devoted to an old man's bed!

DIANA.
That is already answer'd. He's my husband.
You are old, too, my lord.

LETOY.   Yes, but of better metal: 80
A jealous old man, too, whose disposition
Of injury to beauty and young blood
Cannot but kindle fire of just revenge
In you, if you be woman, to requite
With your own pleasure his unnatural spite.   85
You cannot be worse to him than he thinks you,
Considering all the open scorns and jeers
You cast upon him, to a flat defiance;
Then the affronts I gave to choke his anger;
And lastly your stol'n absence from his chamber: 90
All which confirms (we have as good as told him)
That he's a cuckold. Yet you trifle time
As 'twere not worth the doing.

DIANA.   Are you a lord?
Dare you boast honor, and be so ignoble?
Did not you warrant me upon that pawn   95
Which can take up no money, your blank honor,
That you would cure his jealousy, which affects him
Like a sharp sore, if I to ripen it
Would set that counterfeit face of scorn upon him,

---

95. *warrant*] promise.
96. *blank*] "mere, bare, simple" (*OED*).

Only in show of disobedience, which   100
You won me to upon your protestation
To render me unstain'd to his opinion,
And quit me of his jealousy forever.
LETOY.
No, not unstain'd, by your leave, if you call
Unchastity a stain. But for his yellows,   105
Let me but lie with you, and let him know it,
His jealousy is gone, all doubts are clear'd,
And for his love and good opinion,
He shall not dare deny't. Come, be wise,
And this is all; all is as good as done   110
To him already. Let't be so with us;
And trust to me, my power, and your own
To make all good with him. If not: now mark,
To be reveng'd for my lost hopes (which yet
I pray thee save), I'll put thee in his hands,   115
Now in his heat of fury, and not spare
To boast thou art my prostitute, and thrust ye
Out of my gates, to try't out by yourselves.
DIANA.
This you may do, and yet be still a lord;
This can I bear, and still be the same woman!   120
I am not troubled now. Your wooing oratory,
Your violent hands (made stronger by your lust),
Your tempting gifts, and larger promises
Of honor and advancements were all frivolous;
But this last way of threats, ridiculous   125
To a safe mind that bears no guilty grudge.
My peace dwells here, while yonder sits my judge,
And in that faith I'll die.

[V.vi]   *Enter* Joyless *and* Byplay.

LETOY [*aside*].
She is invincible!

V.vi] *Scene number om. in Q.*   0.1.] *Q prints in margin at right of*
                                        l. 1.

___

105. *yellows*] jealousy.   118. *try't out*] thrash it out.
126. *grudge*] "murmuring" or "complaining" of the conscience (*OED*).

Come, I'll relate you to your husband.

JOYLESS.   No,
    I'll meet her with more joy than I receiv'd
    Upon our marriage day. My better soul,
    Let me again embrace thee.

BYPLAY.   Take your dudgeon, sir,   5
    I ha' done you simple service.

JOYLESS.   Oh, my lord,
    My lord, you have cur'd my jealousy, I thank you;
    And more, your man for the discovery;
    But most the constant means, my virtuous wife,
    Your medicine, my sweet lord.

LETOY.   She has ta'en all   10
    I mean to give her, sir. [*To* Byplay.] Now, sirrah, speak.

BYPLAY.
    I brought you to the stand from whence you saw
    How the game went.

JOYLESS.   Oh my dear, dear Diana.

BYPLAY.
    I seem'd to do it against my will, by which I gain'd
    Your bribe of twenty pieces.

JOYLESS.   Much good do thee.   15

BYPLAY.
    But I assure you, my lord give me order
    To place you there after it seems he had
    Well put her to't within.

JOYLESS.   Stay, stay, stay, stay;
    Why may not this be then a counterfeit action,
    Or a false mist to blind me with more error?   20
    The ill I fear'd may have been done before,
    And all this but deceit to daub it o'er.

DIANA.
    Do you fall back again?

JOYLESS.   Shugh, give me leave.

BYPLAY.
    I must take charge, I see, o'th' dagger again.

---

3. *receiv'd*] i.e., received her with.
5. *dudgeon*] knife or dagger with a handle of wood (dudgen).
15. *pieces*] cf. III.ii.48, n.   15. *do thee*] i.e., may it do thee.

LETOY.

 Come, Joyless, I have pity on thee; hear me.   25
 I swear upon mine honor she is chaste.

JOYLESS.

 Honor! An oath of glass!

LETOY.   I prithee, hear me.
 I tried and tempted her for mine own ends,
 More than for thine.

JOYLESS.   That's easily believ'd.

LETOY.

 And had she yielded, I not only had   30
 Rejected her (for it was ne'er my purpose,
 Heaven I call thee to witness, to commit
 A sin with her), but laid a punishment
 Upon her, greater than thou couldst inflict.

JOYLESS.

 But how can this appear?   35

LETOY.

 Do you know your father, lady?

DIANA.

 I hope I am so wise a child.

LETOY [to Byplay].   Go call
 In my friend Truelock.

BYPLAY [to Joyless]. Take your dagger, sir;
 Now I dare trust you.

LETOY.   Sirrah, dare you fool
 When I am serious? Send in Master Truelock. Exit Byplay. 40

DIANA.

 That is my father's name.

JOYLESS.   Can he be here?

LETOY.

 Sir, I am neither conjurer nor witch,
 But a great fortuneteller, that you'll find
 You are happy in a wife, sir, happier—yes,
 Happier by a hundred thousand pound   45
 Than you were yesterday.

JOYLESS.   So, so, now he's mad.

LETOY.

 I mean in possibilities: provided that

---

43. *that*] who says that (Baker).

You use her well, and never more be jealous.
JOYLESS.

Must it come that way.
LETOY.   Look you this way, sir,

When I speak to you; I'll cross your fortune else,   50
As I am true Letoy.
JOYLESS.   Mad, mad, he's mad.

Would we were quickly out on's fingers yet.
LETOY.

When saw you your wife's father? Answer me?
JOYLESS.

He came for London four days before us.
LETOY.

'Tis possible he's here then; do you know him?   55

[V.vii]   *Enter* Truelock.

DIANA.

Oh, I am happy in his sight. Dear sir.   *She kneels.*
LETOY.

'Tis but so much knee labor lost. Stand up,
Stand up, and mind me.
TRUELOCK.   You are well met, son Joyless.
JOYLESS.

How have you been conceal'd, and in this house?
Here's mystery in this.
TRUELOCK.   My good lord's pleasure.   5
LETOY.

Know, sir, that I sent for him, and for you,
Instructing your friend Blaze, my instrument,
To draw you to my doctor with your son.
Your wife, I knew, must follow. What my end
Was in't shall quickly be discover'd to you   10
In a few words of your supposed father.

V.vii] *Q prints scene division (mis-*   1. S.D.] *Q prints in margin at right*
numbered Sc. 6.) *in margin at right of*   *of l. 2.*
V.vi.54.   4. in] *Baker; not in Q.*
0.1.] *Q prints in margin at right of l. 1.*

52. *out on's fingers*] out of his clutches.

DIANA.
    Supposed father!
LETOY.   Yes, come, Master Truelock,
    My constant friend of thirty years' acquaintance,
    Freely declare with your best knowledge now
    Whose child this is.
TRUELOCK.   Your honor does as freely   15
    Release me of my vow, then, in the secret
    I lock'd up in this breast these seventeen years
    Since she was three days old.
LETOY.   True, Master Truelock.
    I do release you of your vow; now speak.
TRUELOCK.
    Now she is yours, my lord, your only daughter;   20
    And know you, Master Joyless, for some reason
    Known to my lord, and large reward to me,
    She has been from the third day of her life
    Reputed mine, and that so covertly,
    That not her lady mother nor my wife   25
    Knew to their deaths the change of my dead infant,
    Nor this sweet lady. 'Tis most true we had
    A trusty nurse's help and secrecy
    Well paid for in the carriage of our plot.
LETOY.
    Now shall you know what mov'd me, sir. I was   30
    A thing beyond a madman, like yourself
    Jealous; and had that strong distrust, and fancied
    Such proofs unto myself against my wife
    That I conceiv'd the child was not mine own,
    And scorn'd to father it; yet I gave to breed her   35
    And marry her as the daughter of this gentleman
    (Two thousand pound I guess you had with her);
    But since your match, my wife upon her death bed
    So clear'd herself of all my foul suspicions
    (Blest be her memory) that I then resolv'd   40
    By some quaint way (for I am still Letoy)
    To see and try her throughly; and so much
    To make her mine, as I should find her worthy.

42. *throughly*] thoroughly.

And now thou art my daughter and mine heir,
Provided still (for I am still Letoy)   45
You honorably love her, and defy
The cuckold-making fiend, foul jealousy.

JOYLESS.

My lord, 'tis not her birth and fortune, which
Do jointly claim a privilege to live
Above my reach of jealousy, shall restrain   50
That passion in me, but her well-tried virtue;
In the true faith of which I am confirm'd,
And throughly cur'd.

LETOY.   As I am true Letoy,
Well said. I hope thy son is cur'd by this, too.

[V.viii]   *Enter* Barbara.

LETOY.

Now Mistress Blaze! Here is a woman now!
I cur'd her husband's jealousy, and twenty more
I'th' town, by means I and my doctor wrought.

BARBARA.

Truly, my lord, my husband has ta'en bread
And drunk upon't, that under heaven he thinks   5
You were the means to make me an honest woman,
Or (at the least) him a contented man.

LETOY.

Ha' done, ha' done—

BARBARA.   Yes, I believe you have done;
And if your husband, lady, be cur'd, as he should be,
And as all foolish jealous husbands ought to be,   10
I know what was done first, if my lord took
That course with you as me—

LETOY.   Prithee, what cam'st thou for?

BARBARA.

My lord, to tell you (as the doctor tells me)
The bride and bridegroom, both, are coming on
The sweetliest to their wits again.

V.viii] *Misnumbered* Sce. 7. *in Q*.   0.1.] *Q prints in margin at right of l. 1.*

---

5. *drunk upon't*] swore solemnly.

LETOY.   I told you.   15
BARBARA.
    Now you are a happy man, sir, and I hope a quiet man.
JOYLESS.
    Full of content and joy.
BARBARA.
    Content! So was my husband when he knew
    The worst he could by his wife. Now you'll live quiet, lady.
LETOY.
    Why flyest thou off thus, woman, from the subject   20
    Thou wert upon?
BARBARA.   I beg your honor's pardon:
    And now I'll tell you. Be it by skill or chance,
    Or both, was never such a cure as is
    Upon that couple; now they strive which most
    Shall love the other.
LETOY.   Are they up and ready?   25
BARBARA.
    Up! Up, and ready to lie down again:
    There is no ho with them;
    They have been in th' Antipodes to some purpose,
    And now are risen and return'd themselves:
    He's her dear "Per," and she is his sweet "Mat."   30
    His kingship and her queenship are forgotten,
    And all their melancholy and his travels pass'd,
    And but suppos'd their dreams.
LETOY.   'Tis excellent.
BARBARA.
    Now, sir, the doctor (for he is become
    An utter stranger to your son, and so   35
    Are all about 'em) craves your presence,
    And such as he's acquainted with.
LETOY.   Go, sir.
    And go you, daughter.
BARBARA [aside].   Daughter! That's the true trick
    Of all old whoremasters, to call their wenches daughters.
LETOY.
    Has he known you, friend Truelock, too?   40

---

  25. *ready*] dressed.   27. *no ho*] no moderation or restraint.

TRUELOCK.
    Yes, from his childhood.
LETOY.   Go, then, and possess him
    (Now he is sensible) how things have gone,
    What art, what means, what friends have been employ'd
    In his rare cure; and win him, by degrees,
    To sense of where he is; bring him to me;   45
    And I have yet an entertainment for him,
    Of better settle-brain than drunkard's porridge,
    To set him right. As I am true Letoy,
    I have one toy left. Go—and go you; why stayst thou?
                Exeunt Joyless, [Truelock, *and* Diana].

BARBARA.
    If I had been a gentlewoman born,   50
    I should have been your daughter, too, my lord.
LETOY.
    But never as she is. You'll know anon.
BARBARA.
    Neat city wives' flesh yet may be as good
    As your coarse country gentlewoman's blood.   *Exit* Barbara.
LETOY.
    Go with thy flesh to Turnbull shambles! Ho   55
    Within there.

[V.ix]   *Enter* Quailpipe.

QUAILPIPE.
    Here, my lord.
LETOY.   The music, songs,
    And dance I gave command for, are they ready?
QUAILPIPE.
    All, my good lord; and (in good sooth) I cannot
    Enough applaud your honor's quaint conceit
    In the design, so apt, so regular,   5

42–45.] *prose in* Q.   V.ix] *Misnumbered* Sce. 8. *in* Q.
52.] *two lines in* Q: But . . . is./   3–11.] *prose in* Q.
You'll . . . anon./

---

    55. *Turnbull*] Elizabethan corruption of "Turnmill Street" in Clerken-
well, a prostitute's haunt.

So pregnant, so acute, and so withal
Poetice legitimate, as I may say
Justly with Plautus—

LETOY.   Prithee say no more,
But see upon my signal given they act
As well as I design'd.

QUAILPIPE.   Nay not so well,   10
My exact lord, but as they may, they shall.   *Exit.*

LETOY.

I know no flatterer in my house but this,
But for his custom I must bear with him.
'Sprecious, they come already. Now begin.

[V.x]

A solemn lesson upon the recorders. Enter Truelock, Joyless, *and* Diana,
Peregrine *and* Martha, Doctor *and* Barbara; Letoy *meets them.* Truelock
presents Peregrine *and* Martha *to him; he salutes them. They seem to make
some short discourse. Then* Letoy *appoints them to sit.* Peregrine *seems
something amazed. The music ceases.*

LETOY.

Again you are welcome, sir, and welcome all.

PEREGRINE.

I am what you are pleas'd to make me; but withal so
ignorant of mine own condition: whether I sleep, or wake,
or talk, or dream; whether I be, or be not; or if I am,
whether I do, or do not anything; for I have had (if I now   5
wake) such dreams, and been so far transported in a long
and tedious voyage of sleep, that I may fear my manners
can acquire no welcome where men understand themselves.

LETOY.

This is music. Sir, you are welcome; and I give full power

V.x] *Misnumbered* Sce. 9. *in* Q.

---

7. *Poetice*] poetically.   13. *custom*] because it is his way (Baker).
14. *'Sprecious*] Cf. II.vii.66, n.
[V.x]
0.1. *lesson*] musical composition or piece to be performed.
0.1. *recorders*] "a wind instrument of the flute kind" (*OED*).

unto your father and my daughter here, your mother, to   10
make you welcome.

Joyless *whispers* [*to*] Peregrine.

PEREGRINE.

How! Your daughter, sir?

DOCTOR [*aside*].

My lord, you'll put him back again if you trouble his brain
with new discoveries.

LETOY [*aside*].

Fetch him you on again then; pray, are you Letoy or I?—   15

JOYLESS.

Indeed it is so, son.

DOCTOR [*aside*].

I fear your show will but perplex him, too.

LETOY [*aside*].

I care not, sir; I'll have it to delay
Your cure a while, that he recover soundly.—
Come, sit again; again you are most welcome.   20

[V.xi]

A most untunable flourish. Enter Discord *attended by* Folly, Jealousy,
Melancholy *and* Madness.

LETOY.

There's an unwelcome guest, uncivil Discord, that trains
into my house her followers: Folly and Jealousy, Melancholy
and Madness.

BARBARA.

My husband presents jealousy in the black and yellow
jaundied suit there, half like man and tother half like   5
woman, with one horn and ass ear upon his head.

LETOY.

Peace, woman. — [*To* Peregrine.] Mark what they

18–20.] *prose in Q.*   V.xi] *Misnumbered* Sce. 10. *in Q.*

---

1. *trains*] lures.
4. *presents*] represents.
5. *jaundied*] jaundiced.
6. *horn . . . ear*] Horns were associated with cuckolds; stupidity, with
the ass.

do: but, by the way, conceive me this but show, sir, and
devise.

PEREGRINE.

I think so.   10

LETOY [*aside*].

How goes he back again, now doctor? Sheugh!

DISCORD.   SONG IN UNTUNABLE NOTES

> *Come forth my darlings, you that breed*
> *The common strifes that discord feed:*
> *Come in the first place, my dear Folly;*
> *Jealousy next, then Melancholy.*   15
> *And last come Madness; thou art he*
> *That bear'st th' effects of all those three.*
> *Lend me your aids, so Discord shall you crown,*
> *And make this place a kingdom of our own.*

[V.xii]

They dance. After a while they are broke off by a flourish, and the approach of
Harmony *followed by Mercury, Cupid, Bacchus and Apollo. Discord and
her faction fall down.*

LETOY.

See Harmony approaches, leading on
'Gainst Discord's factions four great deities:
Mercury, Cupid, Bacchus, and Apollo.
Wit against Folly, Love against Jealousy,
Wine against Melancholy, and 'gainst Madness, Health.   5
Observe the matter and the method.

PEREGRINE.   Yes.

8. but, by] *Baker;* but but by *Q*.   2. four] *Baker;* feare *Q*.
V.xii] *Misnumbered* Scene 11 *in Q*.

---

8. *conceive . . . show*] i.e., consider this to be only a show.

9. *devise*] This could be the common seventeenth-century spelling for
"device" meaning here "purpose" or "intention," usually in form of some
creative invention, such as poetry, masques, etc.; or it could be the verb
"devise" used intransitively to mean "consider" or "examine attentively"
(so *OED*).

[V.xii]

4. *Wit*] i.e., Mercury.
4. *Love*] i.e., Cupid.
5. *Wine*] i.e., Bacchus.   5. *Health*] i.e., Apollo.

LETOY.

And how upon the approach of Harmony,
Discord and her disorders are confounded.

HARMONY.   SONG

Come Wit, come Love, come Wine, come Health,
Maintainers of my commonwealth,   10
'Tis you make Harmony complete,
And from the spheres (her proper seat)
You give her power to reign on earth,
Where Discord claims a right by birth.
Then let us revel it while we are here,   15
And keep possession of this hemisphere.

After a strain or two, Discord *cheers up her faction. They all rise and mingle*
in the dance with Harmony *and the rest. Dance.*

LETOY.

Note there how Discord cheers up her disorders
To mingle in defiance with the virtues;
But soon they vanish, and the mansion quit   *Exit* Discord.
Unto the gods of Health, Love, Wine and Wit,   20
Who triumph in their habitation new
Which they have taken, and assign to you;
In which they now salute you, bids you be
                    [Masquers] *salute* [*and*] *exeunt.*
Of cheer; and for it, lays the charge on me.
And unto me y'are welcome, welcome all.   25
Meat, wine, and mirth shall flow, and what I see,
Yet wanting in your cure, supplied shall be.

PEREGRINE.

Indeed I find me well.

MARTHA.   And so shall I,

After a few such nights more.

BARBARA.   Are you there?

Good madam, pardon errors of my tongue.   30

DIANA.

I am too happy made to think of wrong.

LETOY.

We will want nothing for you that may please,

---

8. *confounded*] overthrown.

Though we dive for it to th' Antipodes.

THE EPILOGUE

DOCTOR.

Whether my cure be perfect yet or no,
It lies not in my doctorship to know.   35
Your approbation may more raise the man,
Than all the College of Physicians can;
And more health from your fair hands may be won,
Than by the strokings of the seventh son.

PEREGRINE.

And from our travels in th' Antipodes,   40
We are not yet arriv'd from off the seas;
But on the waves of desperate fears we roam
Until your gentler hands do waft us home.

*Courteous Reader: You shall find in this book more than was
presented upon the stage, and left out of the presentation, for
superfluous length (as some of the players pretended). I thought good
all should be inserted according to the allowed original; and as it was,
at first, intended for the Cockpit stage, in the right of my most   5
deserving friend, Mr. William Beeston, unto whom it properly
appertained; and so I leave it to thy perusal, as it was generally
applauded, and well acted at Salisbury Court.*

Farewell,

RICHARD BROME.   10

FINIS

---

37. *College of Physicians*] founded by Dr. Buts and situated in Knight-
riders street. By favor of Cardinal Wolsey they obtained a Charter with
privileges and immunities, authorizing them to practice "within the Citie
and suburbes of London and within seven myles thereof every way; and
that none but they ... should be permitted to practice within the sayd
district or limits" (Stow, p. 1078).

39. *strokings ... son*] Seven symbolically denoted completion or perfection; the seventh son in the family was supposedly endowed with
supernatural powers (*OED*).

[To the courteous Reader.]

4. *allowed*] Each new play had to be licensed by the Master of the Revels
before it could be performed.

6. *Beeston*] See Introduction, pp. xi–xii.

Appendix

Chronology

Approximate years are indicated by *.

Life and Major Works of Brome

Drake begins circumnavigation of the earth; completed 1580.

1578
John Lyly's *Euphues: The Anatomy of Wit*.

1579
John Fletcher born.
Sir Thomas North's translation of Plutarch's *Lives*.

1580
Thomas Middleton born.

1583.
Philip Massinger born.

1584
Francis Beaumont born.*

1586
Death of Sir Philip Sidney.
John Ford born.

1587
The Rose theater opened by Henslowe.
Marlowe's *TAMBURLAINE*, Part I.*
Execution of Mary, Queen of Scots.
Drake raids Cadiz.

1588
Defeat of the Spanish Armada.
Marlowe's *TAMBURLAINE*, Part II.*

1589
Greene's *FRIAR BACON AND FRIAR BUNGAY*.*
Marlowe's *THE JEW OF MALTA*.*
Kyd's *THE SPANISH TRAGEDY*.*

1590
Spenser's *Faerie Queene* (Books I–III) published.   Birth.*
Sidney's *Arcadia* published.
Shakespeare's *HENRY VI*, Parts I–III,* *TITUS ANDRONICUS*.*

1591
Shakespeare's *RICHARD III.**

1592
Marlowe's *DOCTOR FAUSTUS**
and *EDWARD II.**
Shakespeare's *TAMING OF THE
SHREW** and *THE COMEDY OF
ERRORS.**
Death of Greene.

1593
Shakespeare's *LOVE'S LABOR'S
LOST;** *Venus and Adonis* published.
Death of Marlowe.
Theaters closed on account of
plague.

1594
Shakespeare's *TWO GENTLE-
MEN OF VERONA;** *The Rape of
Lucrece* published.
Shakespeare's company becomes
Lord Chamberlain's Men.
Death of Kyd.

1595
The Swan Theater built.
Sidney's *Defense of Poesy* published.
Shakespeare's *ROMEO AND
JULIET,** *A MIDSUMMER
NIGHT'S DREAM,** *RICHARD
II.**
Raleigh's first expedition to Guiana.

1596
Spenser's *Faerie Queene* (Books IV–
VI) published.
Shakespeare's *MERCHANT OF
VENICE,** *KING JOHN.**
James Shirley born.

1597
Bacon's *Essays* (first edition).
Shakespeare *HENRY IV*, Part I.**

1598
Demolition of The Theatre.
Shakespeare's *MUCH ADO*

ABOUT NOTHING,* *HENRY IV,*
Part II.*
Jonson's *EVERY MAN IN HIS HUMOR* (first version).
Seven books of Chapman's translation of Homer's *Iliad* published.

1599
The Paul's Boys reopen their theater.
The Globe theater opened.
Shakespeare's *AS YOU LIKE IT,**
HENRY V, JULIUS CAESAR.*
Marston's *ANTONIO AND MELLIDA,** Parts I and II.
Dekker's *THE SHOEMAKERS' HOLIDAY.**
Death of Spenser.

1600
Shakespeare's *TWELFTH NIGHT.**
The Fortune theater built by Alleyn.
The Children of the Chapel begin to play at the Blackfriars.

1601
Shakespeare's *HAMLET,** *MERRY WIVES OF WINDSOR.**
Insurrection and execution of the Earl of Essex.
Jonson's *POETASTER.*

1602
Shakespeare's *TROILUS AND CRESSIDA.**

1603
Death of Queen Elizabeth I; accession of James VI of Scotland as James I.
Florio's translation of Montaigne's *Essays* published.
Shakespeare's *ALL'S WELL THAT ENDS WELL.**
Heywood's *A WOMAN KILLED WITH KINDNESS.*
Marston's *THE MALCONTENT.**

Shakespeare's company becomes the
King's Men.

1604
Shakespeare's *MEASURE FOR
MEASURE,* OTHELLO.**
Marston's *THE FAWN.**
Chapman's *BUSSY D'AMBOIS.**

1605
Shakespeare's *KING LEAR.**
Marston's *THE DUTCH COURT-
ESAN.**
Bacon's *Advancement of Learning* pub-
lished.
The Gunpowder Plot.

1606
Shakespeare's *MACBETH.**
Jonson's *VOLPONE.**
Tourneur's *REVENGER'S TRAG-
EDY.**
The Red Bull theater built.
Death of John Lyly.

1607
Shakespeare's *ANTONY AND
CLEOPATRA.**
Beaumont's *KNIGHT OF THE
BURNING PESTLE.**
Settlement of Jamestown, Virginia.

1608
Shakespeare's *CORIOLANUS,*
TIMON OF ATHENS,*
PERICLES.**
Chapman's *CONSPIRACY AND
TRAGEDY OF CHARLES, DUKE
OF BYRON.**
Dekker's *Gull's Hornbook* published.
Richard Burbage leases Blackfriars
Theatre for King's Company.
John Milton born.

1609
Shakespeare's *CYMBELINE;* Son-
nets* published.
Jonson's *EPICOENE.*

1610
Jonson's *ALCHEMIST*.
Chapman's *REVENGE OF BUSSY D'AMBOIS*.*
Richard Crashaw born.

1611
Authorized (King James) Version of the Bible published.
Shakespeare's *THE WINTER'S TALE*,* *THE TEMPEST*.*
Beaumont and Fletcher's *A KING AND NO KING*.
Middleton's *A CHASTE MAID IN CHEAPSIDE*.*
Tourneur's *ATHEIST'S TRAGEDY*.*
Chapman's translation of *Iliad* completed.

1612
Webster's *THE WHITE DEVIL*.*

1613
The Globe theater burned.
Shakespeare's *HENRY VIII* (with Fletcher).
Webster's *THE DUCHESS OF MALFI*.*
Sir Thomas Overbury murdered.

1614
The Globe theater rebuilt.   In service of Jonson as servant.
The Hope Theatre built.
Jonson's *BARTHOLOMEW FAIR*.

1616
Publication of Folio edition of Jonson's *Works*.
Chapman's *Whole Works of Homer*.
Death of Shakespeare.
Death of Beaumont.

1618
Outbreak of Thirty Years' War.
Execution of Raleigh.

1620
Settlement of Plymouth, Massachusetts.

1621

Middleton's *WOMEN BEWARE WOMEN.* *

Robert Burton's *Anatomy of Melancholy* published.

Andrew Marvell born.

1622

Middleton and Rowley's *THE CHANGELING.* *

Henry Vaughan born.

1623

Publication of Folio edition of Shakespeare's *COMEDIES, HISTORIES, AND TRAGEDIES.*

Collaborates with Jonson in *A FAULT IN FRIENDSHIP* (lost).

1625

Death of King James I; accession of Charles I.

Death of Fletcher.

1626

Death of Tourneur.

Death of Bacon.

1627

Death of Middleton.

1628

Ford's *THE LOVER'S MELANCHOLY.*

Petition of Right.

Buckingham assassinated.

Listed among Queen of Bohemia's players in a warrant dated June 30.

1629

THE CITY WIT; * *THE LOVE-SICK MAID* (lost); *THE NORTHERN LASS.*

1631

Shirley's *THE TRAITOR.*

Death of Donne.

John Dryden born.

Answers a petition of complaint by John Bonus on same day it was filed, December 12.

1632

Massinger's *THE CITY MADAM.* *

THE NOVELLA; * *THE NORTHERN LASS* published; *THE QUEEN'S EXCHANGE.* *

1633

Donne's *Poems* published.

Death of George Herbert.

1634

Death of Chapman, Marston, Webster.*
Publication of THE TWO NOBLE KINSMEN, with title-page attribution to Shakespeare and Fletcher.
Milton's Comus.

Writing regularly (but not exclusively) for Company of Red Bull Players.
CHRISTIANETTA* with George Chapman (lost); THE LIFE AND DEATH OF SIR MARTIN SKINK* with Thomas Heywood (lost); THE LATE LANCASHIRE WITCHES with Thomas Heywood; THE APPRENTICE PRIZE* with Thomas Heywood (lost).

1635

Sir Thomas Browne's Religio Medici.

THE SPARAGUS GARDEN.
Signs a contract on July 20 with Salisbury Court Company giving them exclusive right to his plays.
THE NEW ACADEMY.

1636

THE QUEEN AND CONCUBINE.*
Salisbury Court contract, according to Brome, canceled in May.
Seeks aid from William Beeston in August.
Composes THE ANTIPODES for William Beeston.*
Returns to Salisbury Court Company in October.
THE JEWISH GENTLEMAN* (lost); WIT IN MADNESS (lost).

1637

Death of Jonson.

Commendatory verses for Thomas Nabbes's MICROCOSMOS.
Commendatory verses for Thomas Jordan's Poetical Varieties.
Commendatory verses for Shakerly Marmion's Cupid and Psyche.
THE ENGLISH MOOR.

1638

THE DAMOISELLE;* THE ANTIPODES acted.

New contract with Salisbury Court Company in August to continue writing for another seven years but contract is not signed.

1639
First Bishops' War.
Death of Carew.*

Joins William Beeston at Cockpit Theater in May.
A MAD COUPLE WELL MATCHED * Edits Fletcher's *MONSIEUR THOMAS* for publication.

1640
Short Parliament.
Long Parliament impeaches Laud.
Death of Massinger, Burton.

Lawsuit with Salisbury Court. Bill of Complaint on February 12 answered by Brome on March 6.
THE COURT BEGGAR; THE ANTIPODES published; *THE SPARAGUS GARDEN* published.
Verses in John Tatham's *The Fancy's Theater.*
Verses in Humphrey Mill's *A Night Search.*

1641
Irish rebel.
Death of Heywood.

A JOVIAL CREW.

1642
Charles I leaves London; Civil War breaks out.
Shirley's *COURT SECRET.*
All theaters closed by Act of Parliament.

1643
Parliament swears to the Solemn League and Covenant.

1645
Ordinance for New Model Army enacted.

1646
End of First Civil War.

1647
Army occupies London.
Charles I forms alliance with Scots.
Publication of Folio edition of

Commendatory verses in Folio edition of Beaumont and Fletcher's *COMEDIES AND TRAGEDIES.*

Beaumont and Fletcher's *COM-EDIES AND TRAGEDIES*.
1648
Second Civil War.
1649
Execution of Charles I.   Edits *Lacrymae Musarum*.
1650
Jeremy Collier born.
1651
Hobbes' *Leviathan* published.
1652
First Dutch War began (ended   *A JOVIAL CREW* published.
1654).
Thomas Otway born.
1653
Nathaniel Lee born.*   Mentioned as deceased.
                                            FIVE NEW PLAYS published.

1656
D'Avenant's *THE SIEGE OF RHODES* performed at Rutland House.
1657
John Dennis born.
1658
Death of Oliver Cromwell.
D'Avenant's *THE CRUELTY OF THE SPANIARDS IN PERU* performed at the Cockpit.
1659
                                            FIVE NEW PLAYS (second set)
                                            published.

1660
Restoration of Charles II.
Theatrical patents granted to Thomas Killigrew and Sir William D'Avenant, authorizing them to form, respectively, the King's and the Duke of York's Companies.
1661
Cowley's *THE CUTTER OF COL-EMAN STREET*.
D'Avenant's *THE SIEGE OF RHODES* (expanded to two parts).

1662

Charter granted to the Royal Society.

1663

Dryden's *THE WILD GALLANT*.
Tuke's *THE ADVENTURES OF FIVE HOURS*.

1664

Sir John Vanbrugh born.
Dryden's *THE RIVAL LADIES*.
Dryden and Howard's *THE INDIAN QUEEN*.
Etherege's *THE COMICAL REVENGE*.

1665

Second Dutch War began (ended 1667).
Great Plague.
Dryden's *THE INDIAN EMPEROR*.
Orrery's *MUSTAPHA*.

1666

Fire of London.
Death of James Shirley.